Developing

WRITING SKILLS

JOHN DAYUS • TIM AYRES

Heinemann

Heinemann Educational Publishers
Halley Court, Jordan Hill, Oxford OX2 8EJ
a division of Reed Educational and Professional Publishing Ltd

OXFORD MELBOURNE AUCKLAND
JOHANNESBURG BLANTYRE GABORONE
IBADAN PORTSMOUTH NH (USA) CHICAGO

First published 1999

03 02 01 00
10 9 8 7 6 5

ISBN 0 435 10259 1

Original design by Ken Vail Graphic Design, Cambridge

Designed and typeset by Gecko Limited, Bicester, Oxon

Printed and bound in Spain by Edelvives.

The two clear objectives of *Developing Writing Skills* are:
- *development* of writing skills across a range of genres
- effective *differentiation*.

Development of Skills

Many textbooks offer a wide variety of written experiences to pupils. Progression is assumed by the increasingly challenging nature of the written tasks. *Developing Writing Skills* takes this a step further by focusing specifically on *development*, not merely on *practising* writing.

The unit headings represent a range of genres in which pupils are asked to analyse models of writing. They are then given a supported, step-by-step approach to learning the skills and structures required for the genre, through grids, structured note pages, DARTS activities and writing frames.

Differentiation

Activities in the Student Book are supported by worksheets in the Teacher's Support Pack. These are all included on the CD-ROM. The worksheets provide frameworks, tables and grids to guide and support the students in their responses to the activities. The symbol (WS00) in the margin of the Student Book indicates that an activity is supported by a worksheet in the Teacher's Support Pack/CD-ROM.

A number of the worksheets that appear in the Support Pack are differentiated on the CD-ROM. Differentiation does not mean different pupils getting different frameworks for their answers rather that alternative worksheets are provided, offering the same frameworks but with more support for pupils should they need it. This enables all pupils to access the key concepts and skills which are being developed.

Each of the worksheets on the CD-ROM can be customised, allowing for focused differentiation and enabling worksheets to be adapted for the needs of individual pupils. It also means that worksheets can be personalised: generic or imaginary names on the worksheets can be changed to real-life names.

We hope you will find *Developing Writing Skills* to be a valuable addition to your departmental resources.

Tim Ayres and John Dayus

Contents

Section B: Test Practice

A1 Narrative writing

What makes a good story?

Everybody loves a good story! We were told stories when we were very small children and, as we grow up, we continue to be surrounded by them. But what makes a good story?

Activity

To help you answer this question, think about a story from your early childhood that really stands out in your mind. Work in groups of three or four, and try to tell the other people in your group:

WS1

- what **kind of story** it was (funny? sad? frightening?)
- what **happened** in the story
- what you remember about the **characters** in the story
- the **setting** for the story (where it took place)
- why the story is **memorable**.

Try to give as much detail as you can about each of the bullet points.

The main ingredients

So, *what makes a good story*? Three of the main ingredients are:

- **The plot:** this does not have to be very complicated, but you do need a clear idea of what you are trying to do. Are you trying to make people laugh or cry? Are you trying to arouse their curiosity, or are you trying to scare them?
- **Characters:** you have to be able to picture the characters – see them, hear them, believe in them.
- **The setting:** this gives the stage for the characters, a place where they can develop. In some types of story, the setting is particularly important – for instance, in a ghost story.

This unit will focus on how to develop **character** and **setting** in stories. Although **plot** is important, it is these two 'ingredients' which are vital when writing a good story. You may have the most amazing ideas, but if you can't develop your characters and setting, then your story will not be very interesting, no matter how good your plot is. A very simple story, such as 'My First Day at School', can be a good story if the writer creates interesting characters, and a setting in which they can come to life.

Developing character

How do you develop interesting characters in your writing?

Activities

The first draft of an opening to a story is printed below. It is about a teacher called Mrs Jeffries.

1 a Read the draft and then, in the same group as before, discuss what improvements you would make if you could redraft the story.

Draft 1

> I never liked Mrs Jeffries. She was a horrible teacher, and was often really nasty to the students. She was thin and old, and her clothes were old as well. Her skin was very wrinkled. She had black hair and a pair of round spectacles which she wore at the end of her nose. She always carried a stick in her hand. One day, when my friend walked into the class . . .

b Now read through the second draft of the same story opening. What improvements did the writer make in this draft?

Draft 2

Mrs Jeffries was a horrible teacher. She was very thin, and so old she could have been Queen Victoria's nurse.

She always wore a charcoal grey suit, stained with grease and peppered with flakes of her yellow, leathery skin.

Her black hair was pulled into a tight bun on the back of her head, and she would peer at the class through dusty round spectacles which perched on the end of her nose. Often, she carried a stick, which she would rattle against the blackboard, or slap on the desks of unsuspecting pupils.

One day, when my friend walked into class . . .

2 Working by yourself, use a table like the one below, to write down the details that are given in each draft about Mrs Jeffries:

- age
- clothes
- skin
- hair
- spectacles
- stick.

	Draft 1	Draft 2
Age	old . . .	. . . so old she could have been Queen Victoria's nurse.
Clothes		

3 a Write down all the *adjectives* that describe Mrs Jeffries in the second draft. What impression of her do the adjectives give?

b Write down the *verbs* that add to our impression of Mrs Jeffries in the second draft. What impression of her do they give?

4 a Select **three** improvements that have been made in the second draft, and say what you particularly like about them.

b Explain how the writer has improved the *sentences* in the second draft. Think about the length of the sentences, and how the sentences start.

c Explain how the writer has improved the *structure* of the second draft.

> ### Note
>
> An **adjective** gives more information about a noun:
>   She always wore a **charcoal grey** suit.
>
> A **verb** can describe an action, feeling or thought.
>   She always **wore** a charcoal grey suit.

Activities

Look at the character created by Roald Dahl in this extract from his story *The Ratcatcher*. Like all of Dahl's characters, the ratcatcher is described in great detail.

Read the passage carefully and then complete the tasks on the next page.

The Ratcatcher

In the afternoon the ratcatcher came to the filling station.
He came sidling up the driveway with a stealthy,
soft-treading gait, making no noise at all with his feet
on the gravel. He had an army knapsack slung over one
5 shoulder and he was wearing an old-fashioned black
jacket with large pockets. His brown corduroy trousers
were tied around the knees with pieces of white string.

'Yes?' Claud asked, knowing very well who he was.

'Rodent operative.' His small dark eyes moved swiftly
10 over the premises.

'The ratcatcher?'

'That's me.'

The man was lean and brown with a sharp face and two
long sulphur-coloured teeth that protruded from the upper
15 jaw, overlapping the lower lip, pressing it inward. The ears
were thin and pointed and set far back on the head, near
the nape of the neck. The eyes were almost black, but when
they looked at you there was a flash of yellow somewhere
inside them.

20 'You've come very quick.'

'Special orders from the Health Officer.'

'And now you're going to catch all the rats?'

'Yep.'

The kind of dark furtive eyes he had were those of an animal
25 that lives its life peering out cautiously and forever from a
hole in the ground.

'How are you going to catch them?'

'Ah-h-h,' the ratman said darkly. 'That's all accordin' to
where they is.'

30 'Trap 'em, I suppose.'

'Trap 'em!' he cried, disgusted. 'You won't catch many rats
that way! Rats isn't rabbits, you know.'

He held his face up high, sniffing the air with a nose that
twitched perceptibly from side to side.

35 'No,' he said, scornfully. 'Trappin' is no way to catch a rat.
Rats is clever, let me tell you that. If you want to catch 'em,
you got to know 'em. You got to know rats on this job.'

I could see Claud staring at him with a certain fascination.

'They're more clever 'n dogs, rats is.'

40 'Get away.'

'You know what they do? They watch you! All the time
you're goin' round preparin' to catch 'em, they're sittin'
quietly in dark places, watchin' you.' The man crouched,
stretching his stringy neck far forward . . .

1 This description is special because the ratcatcher was so much like a rat
in the way he looked and in what he did. Did you notice all the rat-like
details? Read the passage again and see if you notice any more.

WS4   2 Write down all the similarities between the ratcatcher and a rat under
the following headings:

• What the ratcatcher looked like
• What the ratcatcher did.

Activities

Now create some of your own characters like the ratcatcher.

1 a Start by looking at this picture of a character called Mrs Tabby, a person who runs a cat hotel.

b First, think carefully about what cats look like.

c Then, think about what cats do.

Cats have:
- sleek coats
- thin lips
- pointed ears
- whiskers
- damp noses

Cats:
- purr
- lie in front of the fire
- stretch out on the settee
- play with balls of wool
- wash themselves constantly

2 What other ideas could be added to the notes above? In pairs or groups, try to think of two or three more ideas for each note page.

3 a Working on your own, begin a story in which Mrs Tabby is the main character. You might want to begin like this:

Mrs Tabby lay on the settee in front of the fire. She stretched luxuriously, enjoying the warmth from the flames. Her thin lips seemed to form a half smile, and . . .

Write another 15–20 lines. In your story, use some of the ideas written on the note pages above, and any additional ideas that you thought of in question 2.

b When you have finished the opening to your story, re-read it. Check that you have used adjectives and verbs to create the effect you want. Change any words that are not working well. Also check that you have used a mixture of sentence types.

Here are three more ideas for creating your own 'ratcatcher'-type character:

Larry Lizard – Keeper of the Reptile House

Julius Guppy – Aquarist

Brenda Turk – Turkey Farmer

Follow the same plan as you did with Mrs Tabby, and write about any **one** of these characters. Of course, if you have a better idea of your own, then use that instead!

Aim to write about 20 lines, as if you were writing the opening page of the first chapter of a book about the character.

 Note

- Use **adjectives** to help you to describe your character in detail.
- Try to **vary** your sentence structure.
- Use **paragraphs**.

Developing a setting

In film and on television, every scene requires a **setting**. After all, you never see actors performing in front of a blank screen!

Soap operas like *Coronation Street* or *Eastenders* have a number of sets which are used regularly. For example, in *Coronation Street*, the street (below) is an outdoor set, and the bar of the Rovers Return an indoor set, and there are many different sets which represent people's houses.

Just as a television producer creates a set, a writer also has to create a **setting** – but with words alone. The focus of this section is how to create such a setting.

Gathering details

Start by looking at the set of *Coronation Street*, shown in the photograph above. There are no people in the photograph, but what clues are there about the people who live there, and their lives?

Activities

1   Imagine that you are writing a novel called *Coronation Street*. Write the opening page of the first chapter of the novel in which you introduce the street to the reader for the first time.

Remember to describe the small details. These details are just as important when describing a **setting** as they are when describing a **character**. You might begin like this:

> Getting off the bus, I had my first glimpse of the street.
> It was quite narrow and the road itself was cobbled …

Most of the details you have described so far will have been **visual** details because they are based on the photograph. These details only appeal to the sense of **sight**. The television producer, however, can appeal to people's sense of **hearing** as well.

2 **a** Look at the photograph again. If it was quite early in the morning, and you were standing in the middle of the street, what sounds would you be likely to hear?

- A milkman whistling?
- The whine of his milk float?
- The rattle of his bottles?
- His footsteps on the cobbles?
- The clunk of the bottles being placed against the wall?

In fact, a writer has a great advantage over a television producer, because a television producer can only appeal to the audience's senses of sight and hearing. A writer can appeal to the reader's other senses too!

  b Think about the following questions:

- What might you **smell**? Bacon frying?
- What about the sense of **touch**? Cold rain on the back of your neck?
- Sense of **taste**? Well, perhaps you might leave that until you're inside a house, having a cup of tea.

  c Take a few minutes to think about these ideas, and then list some of the things that you might notice. Remember, it is seven thirty in the morning, and you are standing in the middle of Coronation Street.

- What might you hear?
- What might you smell?
- What might you feel?
- What might you taste?

Note

You don't *have* to think of something for each heading, of course. On this occasion, it is likely that you will have a number of ideas for the first of these, and perhaps only one or two for the others. In another situation, the reader's sense of smell might be the major sense that you want to appeal to.

The next step is to see how you can weave the sense details you have collected in question 2 into what you have already written about setting for question 1, so that you have a short opening chapter. First, though, look at how another writer has introduced similar details which appeal to the reader's senses.

The passage below is from Penelope Lively's *The Ghost of Thomas Kempe*. In this section, a boy called James, who lives in a village called Ledsham, has woken up in the middle of the night to see a nearby cottage on fire. The author appeals to four senses in the passage: sight, hearing, touch and smell.

3   Read the passage and then discuss with a group or your class how the author appeals to each of those senses.

> He sprang out of bed and dashed to the window. The night was clear and crisp and cold with the moon high now and very bright and Ledsham dark and slumbering underneath, the houses huddled together, their windows curtained and blank. And there was this strong smell of bonfires, and a loud crackling noise as though enormous fingers were rumpling newspaper, and Tim, barking and barking downstairs . . .

4   How are all the different details woven together in this piece of writing? See if you can do the same thing with your work.

You have your first draft of the opening page of the first chapter of *Coronation Street*. You also have your list of sounds, smells, and so on.

Redraft the opening page, weaving in some of the ideas from your list. You should find that you have created a really good opening chapter, one which will help the reader to share your experience as you walk up Coronation Street.

Examining descriptive writing

In the next two passages the authors have described family celebrations.

The first passage is by Jung Chang and is taken from her book *Wild Swans*. In the book, Jung Chang describes what life in China was like for herself, her mother and her grandmother. In the following passage, she describes the excitement, colour and ritual of the Chinese New Year festivities during her mother's childhood.

Read the passage, and then answer the questions on the next page.

At Chinese New Year people gave each other presents. When dawn lit up the white paper in the windows to the east, my mother would jump out of bed
5 and hurry into her new finery: new jacket, new trousers, new socks, and new shoes. Then she and her mother called on neighbours and friends, kow-towing to all the adults. For every bang
10 of her head on the floor, she got a 'red wrapper' with money inside. These packets were to last her the whole year as pocket money.

    The festivities would culminate on
15 the fifteenth day with a carnival procession followed by a lantern show after dark. The procession centred on an inspection visit by the God of Fire. The god would be carried around the
20 neighbourhood to warn people of the danger of fire; with most houses partly made of timber and the climate dry and windy, fire was a constant hazard and

source of terror, and the statue of the
god in the temple used to receive
offerings all year round. The procession
started at the temple of the God of Fire,
in front of the mud hut where the Xias
had lived when they first came to
Jinzhou. A replica of the statue, a giant
with red hair, beard, eyebrows, and
cloak, was carried on an open sedan
chair by eight young men. It was
followed by writhing dragons and lions,
each made up of several men, and by
floats, stilts, and *yangge* dancers who
waved the ends of a long piece of
colourful silk tied around their waists.
Fireworks, drunis, and cymbals made a
thundering noise. My mother skipped
along behind the procession . . .

Questions

1 Which words suggest the excitement that Jung Chang's mother felt?

2 Why does the author keep repeating the word 'new', rather than simply
writing: 'new jacket, trousers, socks, and shoes'?

3 What details does the author include to convey the **colour** and
brightness of the carnival procession?

4 Where does the author refer to the **sounds** of the procession?

5 What **customs** does the author describe in the passage?

The second passage was written by Zahir Hussain (16), a Muslim living in Birmingham. He is describing the Islamic festival, Eid ul-Fitr. This is the festival which brings to an end the month of Ramadan, when Muslims fast, devoting themselves to prayer and eating only during hours of darkness.

Read the passage, and then answer the questions on the next page.

It is the Islamic tradition for men to read Eid Namaaz (Eid prayers) at a mosque, and for women to prepare the food at home. When the men return, the families are united and can celebrate Eid.

5   When I arrived at the mosque in the morning, it had been especially decorated for Eid. Outside, the windows and doors sparkled in the morning sunshine; inside, velvet scrolls bearing inscriptions of Meccan prayers hung from the newly painted walls.

10   The mosque was bustling with men who had acquired soft, smooth complexions after taking their warm morning baths, and many wore new clothes, creating an air of spring freshness about the mosque. After the Namaaz ended, we greeted each other with the traditional saying:

15 'Eid Mubarak' (Eid blessings). I felt honoured in having the chance to read with, and shake the hands of, such experienced and devoted Muslims.

I returned home to discover the vast array of food which my mother and sisters had prepared. It had been laid out on

20 silver plates and trays, all on a clean floor sheet that was covered with Islamic inscriptions and reserved especially for the celebration of Eid. I inhaled the sensuous aroma of soft durum wheat pasta melted in sweet milk (traditionally called *Sehmiah*), with chapatti savoured in butter

25 (*Prahntah*) and small chapatti pieces marinated in sugar and butter (*Choorhi*). There was the sweet aroma of chicken curry flavoured with herbs and spices. There were also many varieties of rice, including sweet rice, which was bright yellow in colour, and savoury rice, cooked with small

30 tender pieces of lamb.

Soon, my brothers arrived with my nephews and nieces. The children grinned and shouted with the excitement of not only receiving new presents, but also with the chance of playing with their cousins, some of whom lived miles away.

35 Their happy faces and eyes lit up the room, which was
drowned with their loud, joyful chants. The place was ablaze
with happiness, as they excitedly danced about.

My brothers and nephews wore traditional Islamic suits,
in bright colours and bearing extravagant embroidered
40 patterns. My sisters and nieces wore yet brighter and more
colourful outfits, and paraded in gold bangles, necklaces and
earrings.

Following Islamic custom, our family ate on the floor,
together and united as one. I sat down next to my mother,
45 as she gave thanks to God for providing us with the food
before us, and for preventing us from experiencing the harsh
difficulties that are part of the everyday life of so many
people.

As everybody began to eat, I paused for a moment.
50 I realised that, unlike so many people, I had the privilege of
sharing my happiness at Eid with those I loved. I was not
going to take it for granted.

by Zahir Hussain

Questions

1 How does the author convey the **colour** and **brightness** of the Eid celebrations?

2 Where does the author refer to the **sounds** of the celebrations?

3 Where does he appeal to the reader's senses of **smell** and **taste**?

4 What **customs** does the author describe in the passage?

Unit summary

Plot

The plot *does not* have to be terribly complicated. But, you *do* need a clear idea of what you are trying to do. Are you trying to make people laugh or cry? Are you trying to arouse their curiosity, or are you trying to scare them? This will play a big part in how you develop your main character. Will the details that you include about the character make them funny, sad, sinister, mysterious or, perhaps, nasty?

Characters

Writers focus on a number of things when developing a character:

- how the person looks – their face and body
- what they wear
- their actions and movements.

There is also another important aspect:

- what they say (dialogue).

The next unit will look at this aspect of writing in detail, but for now, it is worth looking back to *The Ratcatcher* on pages 10–11. What did the ratcatcher's speech tell the reader about him? Read the passage again, and say what the dialogue made *you* feel about the ratcatcher.

Setting

Remember to focus on **small details** when describing a scene.

Try to appeal to all of the **five senses** to help give the reader the atmosphere that you are trying to create in your setting. These are the senses of:

- sight
- hearing
- touch
- smell
- taste.

Adjectives are useful when creating the setting. Adjectives are words which help us to be **precise** when we are writing because they describe what we are writing about.

Activity

Write an account of a festival or celebration that you enjoy.

You could choose one of the following:

- Christmas
- New Year
- Birthday celebrations
- Diwali
- Bonfire Night
- Hanukkah
- Weddings
- Hallowe'en
- Harvest Festival
- End of the school year

Or you might prefer to choose another festival or celebration which you remember very vividly, and write about that.

 Note

Your aim is to convey the colour and excitement of the event to your reader.

Activity

 Now try writing your own story. It can be about anything you choose. It might be a true story about a real person, or it can be completely made up. Remember, though, to keep the plot simple. You should entertain your reader through your ability to bring your main character to life!

- First, think about the **plot**. What kind of story will it be? What will happen in the story?
- Then, **plan** some of the details of your main character. (There is no harm in trying out three or four plans before deciding which one to use in your story.)
- When you have finished your plan, write a **first draft** of your story. As we have seen, you can always improve your story later when you **redraft** your work.
- When redrafting, remember you are especially looking to see if your *details* and *dialogue* tell the reader something about the character. If you set out to arouse the reader's curiosity, for instance, do you think you succeeded?

Dialogue

What is dialogue?

Dialogue in a story is the actual words spoken by the characters. The stories that you write will often be made more lively and interesting by the use of convincing dialogue. Good dialogue can tell us a lot about characters through the things they say and how they say them. There are three main written forms in which dialogue is used:

- in a story
- in a comic strip
- in a play or film script.

Most stories, whether they are in the form of comic strips, stories or plays, contain a mixture of dialogue and narrative. The ways in which the dialogue and narrative are presented are different for each form.

 Note

Punctuating dialogue/speech when writing a story.
- The actual words that someone speaks must be placed within speech marks (speech marks are also called quotation marks). For example:

  'That was a lucky escape,' said Donna.
- Each time there is a change of speaker, you must begin a new paragraph (on the next line, and about 1cm in from the margin). For example:

  'That was a lucky escape,' said Donna.
  'It certainly was,' replied Ricky.
- You must begin with a capital letter every time someone starts to speak.
- You must always put in one of these punctuation marks before the closing speech mark:

  ,   **.**   **?**   **!**

  Comma   Full stop   Question mark   Exclamation mark
- When the speech occurs at the beginning of a sentence, and the sentence continues afterwards, use a comma before the closing speech mark. For example:

  'It certainly was,' replied Ricky. 'Let's leave while we can!'

Dialogue and narrative in stories

In the following passage, Jack and Bridie have got married secretly and are still living separately, with their own parents. It is late at night, two days after the wedding, when Jack makes a decision and drives round to Bridie's house on his motorbike.

Bridie was in bed when Jack arrived. He didn't know whether she slept in the front or the back of the house, so had no way of warning her. He banged on the door and Mr Rooney opened it to him.

5 'What's up?' he asked, not knowing Jack.

'I've c-come for B-B-Bridie.'

'What d'you mean, you've come for bloody Bridie?' The whole house was awake with the man's shouting.

Jack saw her on the stairs, and she gave him strength.

10 'She's my wife.'

He couldn't help smiling, in spite of his terror. Nor could she. Mr Rooney turned round and pulled Bridie down to the door.

'Is it true?'

'Yes, Father,' she whispered. 'We were married on Saturday.'

15 Mr Rooney stared at her, doubt and astonishment and rage chasing each other across his face. A surge of nostalgia swelled up in him. Nothing was dearer to him than romance.

'How old are you, Bridie?' he asked his daughter.

'Twenty-one.'

20 'You're a child yet, for all that,' he said softly. 'You must take care of her, young man.'

He pushed Bridie out on to the doorstep and shut the door before the moisture in his eyes betrayed him.

'But, Father,' said Bridie, hammering on the door. 'I'm still in 25 my nightie.'

'You've made your bed, my girl,' he said roughly, pushing to the bolts on the other side. 'Now you must lie on it.'

'Now what do we do?' asked Bridie.

'We go and tell my parents,' said Jack. 'Together. We should 30 have done it in the first place. We've done it all wrong.'

He took off his jacket and put it round her shoulders, and after a bit of revving and kicking and running up and down the street he got the Matchless started and they set off on the long ride to his parents' house. Bridie snuggled against his back and closed 35 her eyes. He grinned.

'Happy?' he shouted.

She nodded and smiled cosily, even though she knew he couldn't see her doing it. He started singing, with the wind

gasping into his breath and his voice jerking with every rut and
40 stone on the road.

　'I'd like to take you, on a slow boat to China . . .' And Bridie
started laughing, shouting with laughing, and they knew that
nothing as terrible and as wonderful as this would ever happen
to them again.

Granny was a Buffer Girl by Berlie Doherty

Activities

 1　Think about how Berlie Doherty uses dialogue and narrative in this
passage. In particular, what does the way each character speaks tell us
about:

- Bridie
- Jack
- Mr Rooney?

2　a　Berlie Doherty uses a wide range of **reporting clauses** – the words
that tell you *how* a character said something. For example:

'Yes, Father,' she **whispered**.

Why do you think she does this?

　b　Make a list of all the different reporting clauses used in the passage.
What do you think that the effect would be if each piece of direct
speech was followed by 'said'?

You can see that reporting clauses are not used at all in places. For example:

'She's my wife.'
'Is this true?'

When you are writing dialogue, you should aim for a mixture of speech
followed by reporting clauses and speech on its own.

The passage below is taken from the novel *A Kestrel for a Knave* by Barry Hines. Fifteen-year-old Billy Casper has found, reared and trained a kestrel (a type of hawk) and is being persuaded by Mr Farthing, his English teacher, to tell the class about it.

'Now then, Billy, tell me about this hawk. Where did you get it from?'

'Found it.'

'Where?'

5   'In t'wood.'

'What had happened to it? Was it injured or something?'

'It was a young 'un. It must have tumbled from a nest.'

'And how long have you had it?'

'Since last year.'

10   'All that time? Where do you keep it?'

'In a shed.'

'And what do you feed it on?'

'Beef. Mice. Birds.'

'Isn't it cruel though, keeping it in a shed all the time? Wouldn't

15 it be happier flying free?'

Billy looked at Mr Farthing for the first time since he had told him to sit down.

'I don't keep it in t'shed all t'time. I fly it every day.'

'And doesn't it fly away? I thought hawks were wild birds.'

20   ' 'Course it don't fly away. I've trained it.'

Billy looked round, as though daring anyone to challenge his authority.

'Trained it? I thought you'd to be an expert to train hawks.'

'Well I did it.'

25   'Was it difficult?'

' 'Course it was. You've to be right . . . right patient wi' 'em and take your time.'

Activities

1   Look at Billy's speech. It has been written using **non-Standard (colloquial) English**. Re-write it using **Standard English**. What difference does this make to the passage?

2   With a partner, discuss the effectiveness of the dialogue in this passage, and then compare it with the dialogue in the extract from *Granny was a Buffer Girl* on pages 24–25.

Write down your comments under the headings listed below:
- Use of dialogue
- Use of non-Standard English
- Use of reporting clauses
- Use of narrative
- Use of dialect
- Other features

Creating effective dialogue

In both the passages you have studied in this unit so far, the authors have used dialogue to bring their characters to life. This does not always mean that the writing is grammatically accurate or that all the punctuation rules have been obeyed – in fact, sometimes it *isn't* grammatically correct. However, the dialogue *is* realistic or **authentic**. In other words, you can easily imagine people in real-life situations using those words and speaking in that way.

Note

In order to make your dialogue authentic and therefore more effective, you need to think about the following:

- Using colloquial, informal language when appropriate.

- Using a range of techniques to vary the way you set out your dialogue (for example, the use/non-use of reporting clauses).

- Making the characters you create realistic and true to life. Do they, for example, have any speech mannerisms or words they keep repeating? Make sure the opinions they hold reflect their personalities.

- How would a character react in certain situations? For example, when Jack meets Bridie's father in Berlie Doherty's book, it seems that he becomes very nervous because he begins to stammer:

  'I've c-come for B-B-Bridie.'

  It is the attention to small details like this which helps to create effective dialogue.

- Presenting your writing clearly, and remembering all the rules of punctuation!

Activity

Now continue the story of Bridie and Jack when they get to Jack's house and are greeted by his parents (who also don't know that the young couple are married).

Imagine how they would react to Jack turning up very late at night, with his 'wife' dressed in a nightie, on the back of his motorbike. Try to write in the style of the original.

Dialogue and narrative in comic strips

*In a comic strip, you can see at a glance which character is speaking because of the **speech bubble** which points towards them.*

This is not the only way, however, in which information is given to the audience.

***Thought bubbles** show what a character is thinking.*

More information can be gained from the illustrations themselves. They give information about:

The characters:
- what they look like
- what they are wearing
- how they are reacting to people and events around them.

The setting:
- the sort of place where the action is happening.

If the contents of a comic strip were changed into a written story, there would be two main parts:

- the words spoken by the characters would be the **dialogue**
- everything else – the illustrations of events and people – would be the **narrative**.

The dialogue and narrative combine to make up the story.

An example of a comic strip

Look at and read the comic strip on pages 30–31. It is taken from *The Colour of Magic*, a graphic novel by Terry Pratchett. Rincewind the wizard has been persuaded to look after Twoflower, the first-ever tourist to visit the Discworld. Rincewind is not happy with the arrangement.

When you have read it, work through the following questions and activities.

Questions

Discuss the questions below with a partner before writing down your answers.

1 In the largest frame, frame 1, what purpose do the words in rectangular boxes serve?

2 Look carefully at frames 2–5. How would you describe Rincewind's mood? What evidence did you use to reach that view?

3 Why do you think some words are in bold type?

4 Which do you consider to be more important for telling the story – the illustrations or the dialogue?

5 Look at frames 3 and 4. In what tone of voice do you think Twoflower is speaking to Rincewind?

Activities

1 **a** Look at the first three frames in the comic strip. Jot down any words or phrases which describe what you see. Try to include as much detail as you can.

   b Now try to convert those frames into an extract from a narrative story, using words instead of illustrations to paint a picture in the reader's mind of what happens. Use the actual words that are spoken as part of the dialogue, and remember to vary the ways in which you set out your dialogue. The two travellers are on their way from the city of Ankh-Morpork to a town called Chirm.

2 Re-read the extract from *Granny was a Buffer Girl*, by Berlie Doherty, on pages 24–25. Draw a comic strip of six frames to show the events and dialogue which are described. You may have to cut out some of the dialogue in order to fit the whole episode into the frames.

PICTURESQUE.

THAT WAS *A NEW* WORD TO RINCEWIND THE WIZARD (B. MGC, UNSEEN UNIVERSITY [FAILED]). ONE OF A NUMBER HE HAD PICKED UP SINCE LEAVING THE *CHARRED RUINS* OF ANKH-MORPORK.

QUAINT WAS ANOTHER.

'PICTURESQUE' MEANT--

--HE DECIDED AFTER CAREFUL OBSERVATION OF THE *SCENERY* THAT INSPIRED *TWOFLOWER* TO USE THE WORD--

--HORRIBLY PRECIPITOUS.

'QUAINT', WHEN USED TO DESCRIBE THE *VILLAGES* THROUGH WHICH THEY PASSED, MEANT FEVER-RIDDEN AND TUMBLEDOWN.

TWOFLOWER WAS A *TOURIST*, THE FIRST EVER SEEN ON THE DISCWORLD. 'TOURIST', RINCEWIND DECIDED, MEANT...

IDIOT!

THE SENDING OF EIGHT

ADAPTED BY: SCOTT ROCKWELL
PAINTED BY: STEVEN ROSS
LETTERED BY: VICKIE WILLIAMS
EDITED BY: DAVID CAMPITI

HE'S OBVIOUSLY *INSANE*. 'COURSE, HE'S ALSO GENEROUS AND LESS LETHAL THAN HALF THE PEOPLE I MIXED WITH IN THE CITY. I RATHER LIKE HIM.

DISLIKING HIM WOULD BE LIKE KICKING A PUPPY.

IT ALL SEEMS, WELL, RATHER *USELESS* TO ME...

HUH *?* WHA--*!?*

MAGIC...

I ALWAYS THOUGHT THAT A WIZARD JUST SAID THE *MAGIC WORDS* AND THAT WAS THAT.

NOT ALL THIS TEDIOUS *MEMORIZING*.

WELL, MAGIC ISN'T *WILD* LIKE IT WAS IN THE TIME OF THE OLDEN ONES. IT'S BEEN TAMED.

IT HAS TO OBEY THE LAW OF *CONSERVATION OF REALITY*.

SOME OF THE ANCIENT MAGIC CAN STILL BE FOUND IN ITS *RAW STATE*...

--YOU CAN RECOGNIZE IT BY THE SHAPE IT MAKES IN THE *CRYSTALLINE* STRUCTURE OF SPACE-TIME. IT HAS TWICE AS MANY SIDES AS A SQUARE.

IT'S ALL RATHER *DEPRESSING*.

Dialogue and narrative in play and film scripts

There is very little narrative in a film or play script. **Stage directions** and **scene headings** give the reader of a script some information about the narrative, but most of what the writer wants you to know Is conveyed through words spoken by the characters.

Stage directions

These tell you what the characters need to do, how to speak their lines (e.g. *angrily*, *softly*) and where to be on stage. They are written in the present tense.

Scene headings

These tell you where the scene takes place and, perhaps, a little background information. They are also written in the present tense.

Look at this short passage from the beginning of a famous play – *Macbeth*:

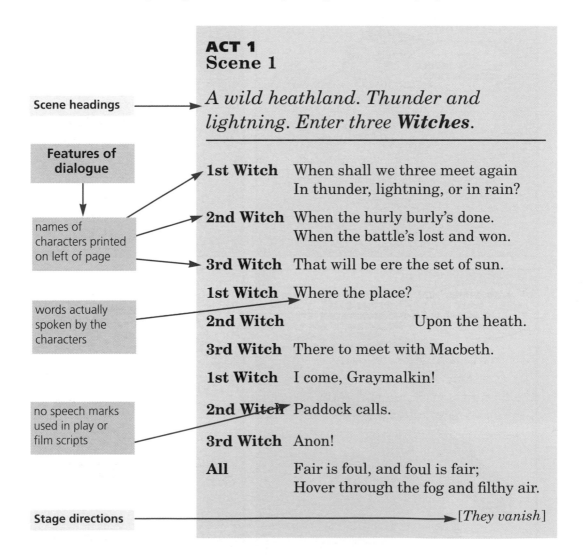

ACT 1
Scene 1

A wild heathland. Thunder and lightning. Enter three **Witches**.

Scene headings

Features of dialogue

names of characters printed on left of page

1st Witch	When shall we three meet again In thunder, lightning, or in rain?
2nd Witch	When the hurly burly's done. When the battle's lost and won.
3rd Witch	That will be ere the set of sun.
1st Witch	Where the place?
2nd Witch	Upon the heath.
3rd Witch	There to meet with Macbeth.
1st Witch	I come, Graymalkin!
2nd Witch	Paddock calls.
3rd Witch	Anon!
All	Fair is foul, and foul is fair; Hover through the fog and filthy air.

words actually spoken by the characters

no speech marks used in play or film scripts

Stage directions → *[They vanish]*

Activity

Look again at the sequence of frames from the graphic novel, *The Colour of Magic*, on pages 30–31.

Imagine that you have been asked to convert this novel into a play script.

The first few lines might look like this:

> ## Scene Four
>
> *A narrow mountain path overlooking a village far below.*
> *Rincewind and Twoflower on horseback followed by packing case.*
> *Twoflower looking at scenery. Rincewind looking miserable.*
>
> **Twoflower** It all seems, well, rather useless to me . . .
>
> **Rincewind** [*Startled out of his thoughts*] Huh? Wha– [*He looks round quickly at Twoflower*]
>
> **Twoflower** Magic. I always thought that a wizard just said the magic words and that was that. Not all this tedious memorizing.
>
> **Rincewind** [*Seriously and patiently*] Well, magic isn't wild like it was in the time of the olden ones. It's been tamed. It has to obey the law of conservation of reality. Some of the ancient magic can still be found in its raw state – you can recognize it by the shape it makes in the crystalline structure of space-time. It has twice as many sides as a square. [*Slowing down speech and horse and looking more miserable*] It's all rather depressing.

Your task is to carry on this script. You will notice that in the final frame, the two men have come to a bridge across the ravine. You will have to decide what happens here. Do they cross the ravine, or carry on up the same side?

Use your imagination to invent both dialogue and a narrative in the form of stage directions. You could introduce other characters if you wish.

Unit summary

In this unit you have learned:

- **Dialogue** and **narrative** are key elements in many stories.
- **Direct speech** must be punctuated correctly.
- **Reporting clauses** can be used to vary the dialogue.
- How to create effective dialogue.
- **Stage directions** and **scene headings** work as the narrative in scripts.
- How to use and adapt dialogue in **comic strips**, **prose** and **scripts**.

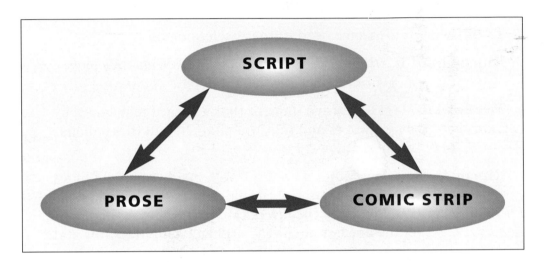

Activity

Your final activity in this unit is to choose a story with which you are familiar and which contains some dialogue. It may be:

- a story you have written yourself
- one you have read
- one you have seen on television or at the cinema.

Your task is to convert a section of the story containing dialogue into the two other forms you have studied.

For example, if you choose a section of *Romeo and Juliet* which is written as a script, you will have to convert this into a comic strip and a piece of prose writing.

If you choose part of a comic strip, then you will have to convert it into a piece of prose and a script.

If you choose a piece of prose, then you will have to convert it into a script and a comic strip.

A3 Writing poetry

What is poetry?

Mention the word 'poetry', and everyone has their own idea of what poetry is:

> Poems rhyme.

> They're about love, often.

> They're often funny, but with a serious side to them.

> It's full of lovely detailed description . . .

> Poems are a bit like photographs, a sort of snapshot of a moment.

> They're usually quite sad.

> Poets write about big events, like battles, or deaths, or disasters . . .

> Poets write about trees and fields and lambs and things . . .

> Poets write about things that make them angry, or make them laugh, or make them cry . . .

> It's like . . . a person's thoughts at a particular time . . .

> It's sort of got a rhythm . . . like a song in a way . . .

> They try to make a point about life . . .

Activities

1   Look at all the comments above, which are people's responses to the question, 'What is poetry?'

2   Think of your own favourite poems. Then, with a partner, look through the responses and pick out three or four that you think are often true *for you*. Remember that you don't have to pick the same responses as your partner does.

WS20 3   After the lesson, try asking a few people how they would describe poetry. You could ask teachers, parents, grandparents, brothers and sisters, friends, etc. Note down their responses and bring them to the next lesson.

Activities

1 Read the three poems below to each other. This can be done in pairs, in groups, or as a whole class.

 2 Take each poem in turn. Look back to page 35, and note down which descriptions you think fit which poems. You may think that more than one description fits a poem.

3 Discuss your findings with a larger group, or the class as a whole. Did you always share the same views? If not, why not?

Streemin

Im in the botom streme
Which meens Im not brigth

dont like reading
cant hardly write

5   but all these divishns
arnt reely fair
look at the cemtery
no streemin there

by Roger McGough

Goodbye

He said
goodbye.
I shuffled
my feet
5   and kept a close
watch on my
shoes. He was talking
I was listening
but he probably
10   thought I was
not
because I never
even lifted my
head.
15   I didn't want him
to see
the mess mascara
makes when it
runs.

by Carol-Anne Marsh

Silver

Slowly, silently, now the moon
Walks the night in her silver shoon;
This way, and that, she peers, and sees
Silver fruit upon silver trees;
5   One by one the casements catch
Her beams beneath the silvery thatch;
Couched in his kennel, like a log,
With paws of silver sleeps the dog;
From their shadowy cote the white breasts peep
10   Of doves in a silver-feathered sleep;
A harvest mouse goes scampering by,
With silver claws, and silver eye;
And moveless fish in the water gleam,
By silver reeds in a silver stream.

by Walter de la Mare

So, what is poetry? You might think that this form of writing is so varied that it is difficult to pick out any description that is true for *all* poetry. All the descriptions on page 35 will be true for *some* poems, but was there one that could possibly be true of all poems? If not, can you think of one?

There are no hard and fast 'rules' that you have to stick to if you are to write successful poems. Poems are too individual for that. They can be about anything, and they can be written in many different **styles**.

That is not to say that there is nothing to learn. There are poetic techniques and, like a singer, a poet needs to find his own 'voice'. You can do this by trying out lots of different styles.

Using poems as a framework

You are now going to explore the idea of using one poem as a framework for another, quite different, poem.

In the poem below, **images of the ordinary world** (the woodshed, the nest, dandelions, etc.) are mixed with **fantastic images** (the dragon, the roots of stars, etc.) so that the reader shares the child's sense of wonder at this discovery. Read it and then turn to page 38.

A Small Dragon

I've found a small dragon in the woodshed.
Think it must have come from deep inside a forest
because it's damp and green and leaves
are still reflecting in its eyes.

5   I fed it on many things, tried grass,
the roots of stars, hazel-nut and dandelion,
but it stared up at me as if to say, I need
foods you can't provide.

It made a nest among the coal,
10 not unlike a bird's but larger,
it's out of place here
and is quite silent.

If you believed in it I would come
hurrying to your house to let you share my wonder,
15 but I want instead to see
if you yourself will pass this way.

by Brian Patten

The poem, *A Small Dragon,* can be used as a framework for your own poem. All you need to do is put in a few ideas of your own. Look at the following example.

The speaker in *A Small Dragon* has found a dragon in the woodshed. Think about:

- what you might find. This has to be **fantastic**.
  A rainbow, perhaps.
- where you might find it. This needs to be **ordinary**.
  In the garden, perhaps.
- what you might do with it. Again, this should be **fantastic**.
  Make it a crock of gold? Feed it rainwater? Sunshine?

Your poem might look like this:

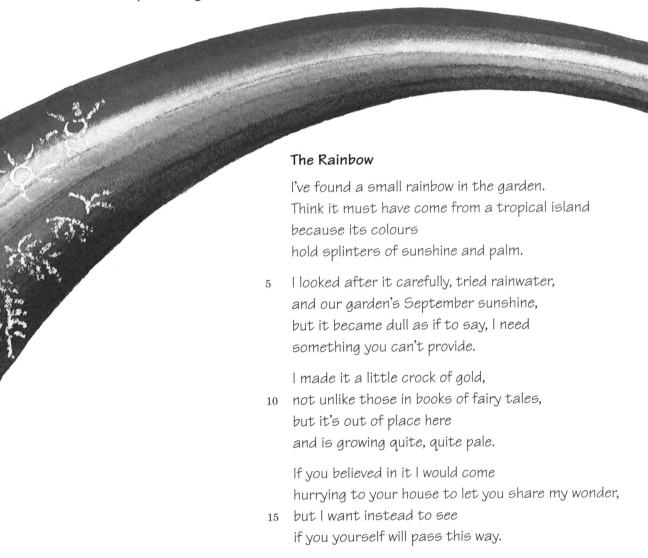

The Rainbow

I've found a small rainbow in the garden.
Think it must have come from a tropical island
because its colours
hold splinters of sunshine and palm.

5 I looked after it carefully, tried rainwater,
and our garden's September sunshine,
but it became dull as if to say, I need
something you can't provide.

I made it a little crock of gold,
10 not unlike those in books of fairy tales,
but it's out of place here
and is growing quite, quite pale.

If you believed in it I would come
hurrying to your house to let you share my wonder,
15 but I want instead to see
if you yourself will pass this way.

Activities

1 Read through *The Rainbow* carefully. Which sections have changed from the first poem, *A Small Dragon,* and which remain the same?

Now create your own poem by using *A Small Dragon* as a framework.

a First, you will need to brainstorm a few ideas. Make a framework like the one below to try some ideas of your own. Use the example on page 38 to help you.

> **Note**
>
> - **what** you find should be **fantastic**:
>   *a dragon, a rainbow, a lion, an ancient king, a star*, and so on.
> - **where** you find it should be **ordinary**:
>   *in the woodshed, in the garden, under the bed, in a cupboard*, and so on.

What could you find?

- A rainbow
-
-
-

Where could you find it?

- In the garden
-
-
-

How would you feed it/look after it?

- Rainwater, September sunshine, crock of gold
-
-
-

What might happen to it?

- It might grow pale
-
-
-

---

b When you have finished the brainstorm, try to develop one of your ideas by drafting out your own poem.

Remember what you considered earlier. Which sections of the poem will you change, and which will you keep unchanged?

3 Use the poem below as a framework for your own poem. Notice how each stanza begins with 'I remember …'. In this way each stanza captures a particular memory that the poet has of a holiday that she enjoyed. Read the poem first.

Holiday

I remember the sea
The sea
Moaning, rumbling, grumbling, roaring,
Playing like a lion on the sinking yellow sands,
5 Pouncing and retreating in a swell of white-green passion
And dying,
Dying.

I remember the night,
Serene above the water, pulsing deep below,
10 In a dark disguise of moonlight
Fluttering over silver sands and fading,
Fading into dimness far away.

I remember the sun,
The burning warmth of human flesh on silky dunes,
15 The gravel heat beneath two weary feet
And the scorched, parched throats,
Choking dry.

I remember the days,
The glorious journeys into the sunset,
20 The sea and nights and sun
The summer heat and weariness and rest
And happiness.

by Corolyn J Turner

When you write your poem you could try two different approaches:

a You could keep the subject matter the same, thinking about things that *you* remember from a holiday that *you* enjoyed.

For example:

> I remember the beach,
> Covering dad with golden sand as he slept,
> Watching the brilliant scarlet kite
> Soar and dive in the playful wind . . .

b You could change the title and, therefore, the focus of the poem.

For example:

> **Starting School**
> I remember
> my mum, when she turned to go . . .

Techniques in poetry

On pages 37–40, you developed your poetry by using another poem as a framework to hold your own ideas.

Now you are going to go on to look at some techniques that poets use from time to time, and try using them to write your own poems.

Using sound

We all use words, thousands of them, every day, but how often do we stop to think about the **sounds** of words?

Activities

Imagine having two bags to keep words in. One bag is for words that you associate with love; the other bag is for words that you associate with hatred.

 1 List at least ten words that you would put in the bag labelled *love*, and ten that you would put in the bag labelled *hatred*.

> For example:
> **love:**   caress, moon, kiss, candlelight . . .
> **hatred:** stab, curse, scream, anger . . .

2 When you have finished, compare your sets of words with those of a partner. What do you notice about how the sets of words about *love* tend to **sound** in comparison with the sets of words about *hatred*?

3 Did you notice the hard sounds of one set of words and the soft sounds of the other? Consider the **consonants** in the alphabet for a moment (consonants are all the letters except **a**, **e**, **i**, **o** and **u**). Which **consonants** would you describe as 'soft', and which as 'hard'? Are there any that you are unsure about?

4 Now you have got two bags of words, try to expand them into poems. Take some of the words that you have put into the bags, and use these as the basis for two new poems. Each poem has been started for you. You do not have to use the openings below if you don't want to; if you prefer, you can start from scratch with your own ideas and develop those.

This bag contains love,
the kiss of candlelight,
the caress of the moon,

....

....

This bag contains hatred,
a stabbing on the empty street,
the bloody curse of anger,

....

....

 WS29 **5** You have been writing about two extreme emotions. Now think of a few more emotions. Choose one from the list below, or one that you have just thought of. Then, collect words for your bag before you go on to expand these into a poem.

- Sorrow
- Pride
- Boredom

- Happiness
- Shame
- Excitement

Note

Will you need words which sound **soft** or **hard** for your poem?

Onomatopoeia and Alliteration

While you are thinking about the **sounds** of words, you should think
about two particular techniques where the sounds of words are important.

1 Onomatopoeia
This is an effect where words actually sound like the noise that they
describe: words like *shuffle*, *whine* and *hiss*.

2 Alliteration
This is an effect created by the same consonant sound being repeated:
*The **w**ind **w**hispered through the grass and **w**ailed in the **w**oods.*

Activities

1 Read the poem below, and note down all the examples of **onomatopoeia**
and **alliteration** you can find.

Huffer and Cuffer

Huffer, a giant ungainly and gruff
encountered a giant called Cuffer.
said Cuffer to Huffer, I'M ROUGH AND I'M TOUGH
said Huffer to Cuffer, I'M TOUGHER.

5 they shouted such insults as BOOB and BUFFOON
and OVERBLOWN BLOWHARD and BLIMP
and BLUSTERING BLUBBER and BLOATED BALLOON
and SHATTERBRAIN, SHORTY and SHRIMP.

then Huffer and Cuffer exchanged mighty blows,
10 they basted and battered and belted,
they chopped to the neck and they bopped in the nose
and they pounded and pummelled and pelted.

they pinched and they punched and they smacked
    and they whacked
15 and they rocked and they socked and they smashed,
and they rapped and they slapped and they
    throttled and thwacked
and they thumped and they bumped and they bashed.

they cudgelled each other on top of the head
20 with swipes of the awfullest sort,
and now they are no longer giants, instead
they both are exceedingly short.

by Jack Prelutsky

2 Now you are going to write a poem called *Ghost*.
- Fill a word bag with ghostly **onomatopoeia**, for example, *sigh*, *clatter*
  and another one with ghostly **alliteration**, for example, *wailed round
  the walls*.
- Now take your words and phrases and try to expand them into a poem.

Using imagery

As well as considering individual words, we also need to think about **imagery**. We use **imagery** in everyday life. For example:

> He woke up **with pins and needles in his hand**.

If he *literally* had pins and needles in his hand, he'd be in agony! This phrase is an **image**, a comparison which tries to capture the feeling in his hand.

Think about this sentence:

> Here at Wembley, as we await the start of the Cup Final, **the atmosphere is electric**.

What the commentator means is that everybody is very excited, but can you see how the image conveys the sense of excitement much more effectively than if he just said, 'Everybody is very excited.'?

Similes

Images are commonly expressed as **similes**. A simile is a comparison of one thing with another, using the key words *as* or *like*. For example:

> When I was sent home from school, **my dad was like a raging bull**.

Metaphors

Images can also be expressed as **metaphors**. A metaphor is when something is described as if it *is* something else. For example:

> He was so thin, **his legs were mere matchsticks**.

Activities

In the notes below, the writer has started with an idea and expanded it into a five-line poem by using similes and metaphors. Read the notes and then work through the activities on page 45.

> **IDEA:** If my mum were a shoe, she'd be . . . a stiletto:
>
> **POEM:** If my mum were a shoe she'd be a stiletto,
>   bright blue or scarlet,
>   smooth like suede,
>   tall and elegant and rather haughty.
>   But out of date like last year's calendar.
>
> **IDEA:** If my dad were a garden he'd be . . . overgrown:
>
> **POEM:** If my dad were a garden he'd be overgrown,
>   dandelions coming through
>   like splodges of pale yellow custard
>   the edges of the lawn no longer neat,
>   the pond murky with fallen leaves.

1   Now see if you can write your own five-line poems like those on the previous page.

   a   Plan your poem first. Divide your page into two columns as below. In the left-hand column, write down possible 'subjects' for poems. In the right-hand column, write down comparisons. A few examples have been given to help you.

Subject	Comparison
Mum	An item of clothing
Dad	A vegetable
My brother	A car
My sister	A building
My friend	A place
Our neighbour	A place
Our dog	Weather

   Remember, you may mix the ideas as much as you like. For instance, you might think of your friend in terms of *any* or *all* of the comparisons in the right-hand column.

   b   Choose the subject you want to write about, and the comparison you will use. Then use similes and metaphors to describe the person in a five-line poem of your own.

2   Another idea is to write a longer poem about a person, going through a series of comparisons. Pick another subject from the list you made in question 1 and try to write a five-line poem like this:

> **My Dad**
> He's an old woolly jumper,
> with holes in the elbows;
> he's a cabbage that's boiled for hours.
> He's a rusted old Skoda.
> He's a shed needing paint.

Personification

One very special form of imagery is called **personification**. This is when an inanimate object is given a human or animal characteristic.

For example:

The wind sighed through the branches and whispered through the leaves.

The signal nodded and the train urged its tired body slowly forward.

In the first example, the wind is given the human characteristics of sighing and whispering. In the second, both the signal and the train are given human characteristics.

In both examples, the effect is once more to take the reader closer to the emotion or feeling of the scene being described.

Read this poem, and then answer the questions below.

Winter

Winter crept
through the whispering wood
hushing fir and oak
crushed each leaf and froze each web
5   but never a word was spoke.

Winter prowled
by the shivering sea
lifting sand and stone;
nipped each limpet silently –
10   and then moved on.

Winter raced
down the frozen stream,
catching at his breath;
on his lips were icicles
15   at his back was death.

by Judith Nicholls

Questions

1   What do you notice about the **first line** of each stanza of the poem?
2   What do you notice about the **second line** of each stanza?
3   How does the poet 'give life' to **Winter**?
4   How does she 'give life' to **the wood** and **the sea**?

Activity

Now try to complete a set of poems called *Seasons*. Your task is to write three more poems to accompany the one above. The three poems will be entitled *Spring*, *Summer* and *Autumn*.

Use the poem above as your model. This means that:

- each poem should have three stanzas
- each stanza should begin with the **season** and a **verb** (e.g. *Spring awoke*)
- the second line of each stanza should name a **place**
- you should try to put forward the **personality** of the season through your use of **personification**.

Unit summary

In this unit you have learned:

- Poetry can be about anything.
- It can take many different forms. There is no form or structure that can be called 'right' or 'wrong' when you are considering poetry.
- **Sounds of words** are very important in poetry. Some words sound soft, while others sound hard. The softness or hardness of the word's sound depends largely on the **consonants** that are used in it.
- **Onomatopoeia** is the effect where a word actually sounds like the noise it describes.
- **Alliteration** is the effect where consonant sounds are repeated for particular effects.
- Images can be expressed as **similes** and **metaphors**. They can sometimes take us nearer to a feeling or an emotion than a literal description could.
- How you can use **personification** to give inanimate objects human or animal characteristics.

Activity

In the course of completing this unit, you have probably worked on four or five of your own poems. Select **two** of these, and read them through.

Now you have completed the unit, would you change them in any way?

Redraft these poems, perhaps using a desktop publishing package to present them in an interesting way. Look through the poetry section in this text book, and in other poetry anthologies, to give you ideas about presentation.

Letters

Letters form an important part of life, especially as you grow older. You may receive several letters a month and will have to write many in your lifetime. There is also a chance that you will have to write a letter of some kind in your SATs or, later on, in your GCSE English exam.

Audience and purpose

When writing a letter, as in any other kind of writing, you will have to consider very carefully:

The audience: *who* the letter is addressed to.

The purpose: *why* you are writing it (e.g. to explain, to inform, to entertain, to persuade, to describe or to express an opinion).

Activities

1 Look at the following extracts from a selection of letters. For each one, see if you can identify
   - the intended audience
   - its purpose (is it to inform, explain, describe, entertain or persuade?)
   - whether the writing is formal or informal.

   Use a table like the one on page 49 to record your answers.

A

and I would also like a pink and white Furby with a mane. That would be really great. I hope that Rudolf is OK. I'll leave a carrot in the usual place by the

B

*as he was feeling unwell and had a high temperature.
He is now much better and well enough to return to school.
Yours sincerely*

C

and when I tried to put on the trousers, imagine my horror when I found they had shrunk by six inches.

I am very unhappy about this situation as I have paid £75 for

D

Dear Mr J Brown
You are one of the lucky few to have been chosen to take part in our fabulous 'Holiday of a Lifetime' Prize Draw. In fact, you may already have won a cash

E

and you should have seen the look on his face – it was priceless!

Are we still meeting in London on the 14th in the usual place? I can't wait to see you

	Intended Audience	Purpose	Formal/Informal
Extract A	Father Christmas		informal
Extract B		to explain	
Extract C	complaints department		
Extract D			formal
Extract E		to inform	

2 Look carefully at extracts D and E. On separate pieces of paper (or on separate pages in your exercise books) write what you imagine the full text of each letter, including the extract given, might have been. You should maintain the style and tone of the original; you will need to use your imagination to make up some details. (You can change the name in extract D to your own name if you wish.)

Formal or informal?

When writing a letter, you have to choose language which fits the purpose and which creates the right overall tone. It is therefore vital that you know the difference between **formal** and **informal language** and know when to use each one.

A formal letter

This is usually written to someone you do not know well (or do not know at all). In this type of letter, you have to use formal language which follows recognizable rules of spelling, grammar and punctuation and is often known as **Standard English**. You should aim to adopt a polite, businesslike tone and try to make your point quickly and concisely.

An informal or personal letter

This is usually written to someone you know – a friend or relation, perhaps. In this type of letter, you should aim to adopt a *friendly* and *conversational* tone, and you can use **slang** expressions occasionally, as long as you know the recipient of the letter will understand them.

 Note

There are many different situations in which you will need to write a letter. You must think carefully about your audience and the purpose for your writing, to help you make the right choice between a formal and an informal letter.

Activity

With a partner, discuss and then write down five situations when you might write a formal letter, and five when you might write an informal letter. Use a table like the one below.

Formal	Informal
1	1
2	2
3	3
4	4
5	5

Layout

There are certain **layouts** you need to use and rules you need to follow when setting out both formal and informal letters.

Activity

Look carefully at the following example of a formal letter.

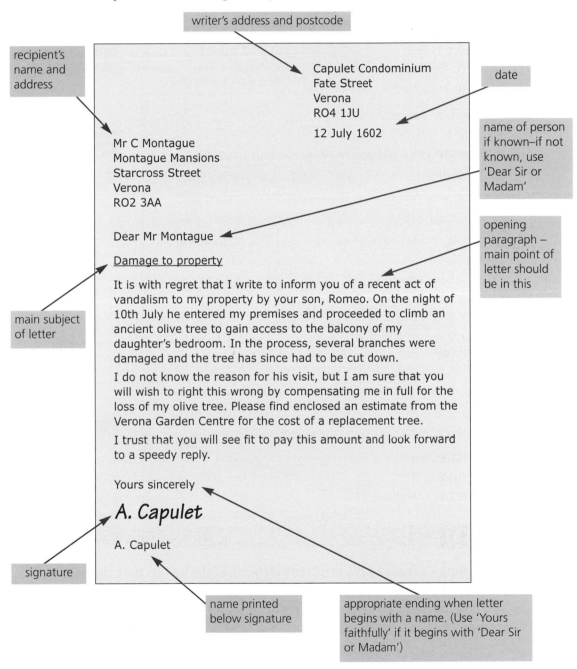

writer's address and postcode

recipient's name and address

date

Capulet Condominium
Fate Street
Verona
RO4 1JU

12 July 1602

name of person if known–if not known, use 'Dear Sir or Madam'

Mr C Montague
Montague Mansions
Starcross Street
Verona
RO2 3AA

Dear Mr Montague

Damage to property

opening paragraph – main point of letter should be in this

main subject of letter

It is with regret that I write to inform you of a recent act of vandalism to my property by your son, Romeo. On the night of 10th July he entered my premises and proceeded to climb an ancient olive tree to gain access to the balcony of my daughter's bedroom. In the process, several branches were damaged and the tree has since had to be cut down.

I do not know the reason for his visit, but I am sure that you will wish to right this wrong by compensating me in full for the loss of my olive tree. Please find enclosed an estimate from the Verona Garden Centre for the cost of a replacement tree.

I trust that you will see fit to pay this amount and look forward to a speedy reply.

Yours sincerely

A. Capulet

A. Capulet

signature

name printed below signature

appropriate ending when letter begins with a name. (Use 'Yours faithfully' if it begins with 'Dear Sir or Madam')

WS33-34 Using this letter as a model for layout and tone, write a formal letter of reply to Mr Capulet from Mr Montague. You can decide whether or not to pay for the replacement tree!

Activities

1   Look carefully at the following example of an informal letter. Notice that it is hand-written (although of course it could be typed), and that the first line of each paragraph is set in from the margin. There is no space between the paragraphs either. Compare the way typed paragraphs are laid out, on page 51.

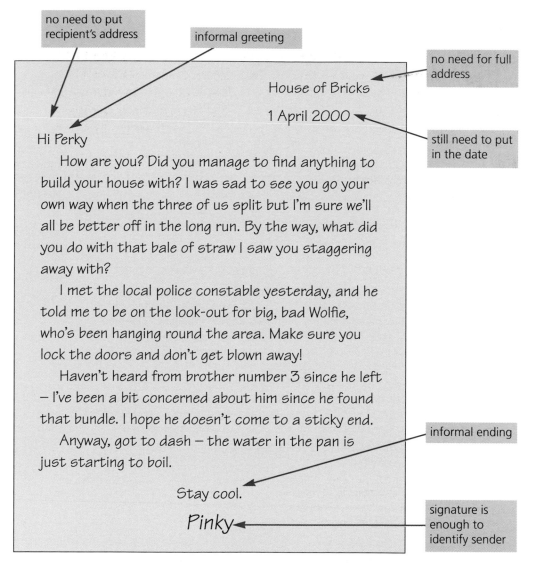

no need to put recipient's address

informal greeting

no need for full address

House of Bricks

1 April 2000

still need to put in the date

Hi Perky

How are you? Did you manage to find anything to build your house with? I was sad to see you go your own way when the three of us split but I'm sure we'll all be better off in the long run. By the way, what did you do with that bale of straw I saw you staggering away with?

I met the local police constable yesterday, and he told me to be on the look-out for big, bad Wolfie, who's been hanging round the area. Make sure you lock the doors and don't get blown away!

Haven't heard from brother number 3 since he left – I've been a bit concerned about him since he found that bundle. I hope he doesn't come to a sticky end.

Anyway, got to dash – the water in the pan is just starting to boil.

Stay cool.

informal ending

Pinky

signature is enough to identify sender

WS35 2   Write Perky's reply to his brother's letter (before he has met the wolf!). This will be an informal, personal letter. Try to make it as humorous as you can, perhaps by telling Pinky not to worry about your house of straw.

WS36 3   It is now a few weeks later. Pinky's two brothers, Perky and Porky, were forced out of their houses by the wolf, and have gone to live with Pinky. The wolf has now finally been dealt with! Imagine you are one of the three little pigs. Write an informal letter home to your mother, outlining what has happened.

Language

As well as choosing the right **layout** for the sort of letter you want to write, you must use the appropriate sort of **language** too. You probably noticed that the language in the letter on page 52 was very similar to how someone might talk every day – it was **informal**; the language in the letter on page 51, on the other hand, was **formal**.

Activities

Read the letter below and the one on page 54 carefully. They were both written by Monty Tyler, a sixteen-year-old pupil who lives in Manchester and who will be taking his exams in May. One of the letters was written home to his parents while he was on a field trip in Cornwall, and the other was written to a local supermarket as an application for a Saturday job.

Unfortunately, Monty has not had much practice at writing letters, and doesn't really know much about layout or when to use formal and informal language.

A   Monty's letter to his parents

> Bodmoor Study Centre
> Exerby
> Cornwall
> EX17 7JL
>
> 10 March 2000
>
> Mr & Mrs R Tyler
> 46 High Street
> Mossbrook
> Manchester
> M24 6QT
>
> Dear Sir and Madam
>
> I am writing this letter to let you know that I arrived safely and that the accommodation in which I am residing is satisfactory. The journey down here was comfortable, and I have just finished unpacking my belongings.
>
> I do hope that this letter finds you in good spirits, and that the recent attack of influenza suffered by Mrs Tyler has receded.
>
> As mentioned in our recent telephone conversation, I should be grateful if you would feed my pet goldfish until my return.
>
> I confirm that I will be returning home on 17th March, and look forward to meeting you both then.
>
> Yours faithfully
>
> *M Tyler*
>
> M Tyler

B   Monty's letter of application to the supermarket

> Home
>
> Friday night
>
> Dear Jenny
>
> Thought I'd write to apply for the job you advertised last week. I'm a bit skint at the moment and working in your supermarket would be really good - I only live round the corner so it'd be dead handy for me.
>
> I get on with people - well most of the time anyway - and I'm good at sums using a calculator so I think it would suit me down to the ground.
>
> Give me a ring when you want me to start.
>
> Cheers
>
> Monty

1 Monty has asked his English teacher to look at the letters and advise him how to improve them. Imagine you are that teacher. Write a detailed explanation of what Monty has got wrong in each letter. Suggest ways in which he can put them right under the headings:

- Tone
- Language
- Layout

2 Re-write each letter using the correct tone, language and layout. You may if you wish make up other details to make the letters more authentic and appropriate to their purpose.

Letters of complaint

There may be many occasions when you wish to write a letter of complaint: the CD you ordered is damaged when it arrives; the shoes you bought last week begin to disintegrate; the 'male' hamster sold to you by the pet shop has babies!

Whatever the reason, there are some simple rules when writing a letter of complaint which will help you to get the best results.

1   Think first about the *audience* and *purpose* of your letter

The **audience** could be the manager of a shop or the complaints department of a large firm or company, but – whoever it is – you should treat this as a *formal* letter and write in Standard English.

The **purpose** of the letter depends upon the nature of the complaint, but you should have a clear idea of what you would like to happen as a result of your letter. You might wish to have an item replaced, receive a refund, or even just get a letter of apology. Keep your purpose in mind as you write the letter.

2   Be relevant

The person to whom you are writing may know nothing about your complaint. You need to explain it to them, and keep their interest while you do so. You should therefore try to be clear, stick to the point and avoid irrelevant details. This will also help you to follow the next important rule about writing a letter of complaint.

3   Be brief

A ten-page letter giving every little detail might be very accurate, but the person reading the letter may be extremely busy; you want them on your side, so stick to the main facts and keep the letter as short as possible.

4   Be polite

Don't give in to the temptation to insult the shop or person who dealt with you. You may well feel very strongly about what has happened, but it is always better to keep your emotions under control – you will probably write a more effective letter as a result!

5   Layout

Use the layout of a formal letter. Including the name of a person or a department will mean that the letter is given to the right person as soon as possible.

Activities

Look at the comic strip on the opposite page and then work through the following activities.

1 Imagine that you are one of the innocent girls who was asked to leave the bus.

You arrive home and immediately sit down to write a letter of complaint about the treatment you have received on the bus today. You look in the telephone directory at the section shown below.

The notes you jotted down about what happened are also given below. Some details, such as a name and address, you can make up for yourself, if you do not want to use your own.

Use the comic strip and information from this unit to help you draft the letter and lay it out.

An extract from the Business Section of the local telephone directory

Midland Archery Consultants, 17 High St., Brimington 8 . . . . 625 3942
Midland Auto Services, 273 Windham St., Brimington 26 . . . . 356 8240
Midvale Bus & Coach Hire, 152 Green Road, Brimington 24 . . . . . 741 8110
Midvale Transport Co., Transport House, High St., Brimington 8 . . . 625 7373
Midvale Truck Co., 22 Acacia Avenue, Brimington 18 . . . . 366 4426

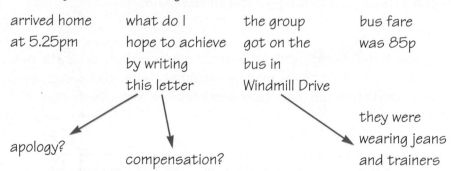

no money left after leaving the bus

arrived home at 5.25pm

what do I hope to achieve by writing this letter

the group got on the bus in Windmill Drive

bus fare was 85p

apology?

compensation?

they were wearing jeans and trainers

> **Note**
> - try to make the letter as realistic as possible
> - only include relevant details
> - be polite
> - have a clear purpose.

2 Imagine you work in the Complaints Department of the bus company. Reply to the letter, saying what action you will be taking as a result of the complaint.

Unit summary

In this unit you have learned:

- When writing a letter, you must think carefully about **audience** and **purpose**.
- **Formal letters** are usually written to people you don't know well, and have rules which you must follow:
  - put your address in the top right-hand corner
  - write the date underneath your address
  - write the name and address of the person you're writing to on the left-hand side
  - if you begin with *Dear Sir* or *Madam*, then end with *Yours faithfully*
  - if you begin with the name of the person you're writing to, then end with *Yours sincerely*
  - sign the letter, and print your name underneath your signature
  - use Standard English (no slang), be polite and keep to the point.
- **Informal letters** are usually written to friends and family, and do not have strict rules.

  When writing informal letters, however, you should:
  - put the date in the top right-hand corner
  - address the person by name
  - end the letter informally.

Activity

Write a letter to a famous person in history expressing your opinion of them and commenting on one or more aspects of their contribution to history. Make the tone of your letter formal and set the letter out accordingly.

A5 Diaries

What is a diary?

Purpose

A diary is a personal account of what someone thinks, feels or sees in their daily lives. The person who writes the diary is called the diarist.

Diary entries can be particularly interesting to read because they give a personal view of events, situations and people, and often include judgements and opinions as well as facts. Many diary entries are very personal, and are not to be read by a wider audience, while some are written specifically to be read by others.

In fiction, writers can use diaries to increase the reader's understanding of characters.

You can use a diary:
- to express inner thoughts/ideas
- to record situations or a way of life
- to give opinions
- to entertain or interest an audience
- as a record of travels
- as a daily or frequent record of events or any combination of these!

Writing a diary can help you to:
- organize your thoughts
- show how you change over time
- provide a more reliable record than your memory
- document events.

Diaries are very much like informal letters – there are no hard and fast rules to follow. There is, therefore, a great deal of variety in the ways in which diaries are written – some people include a great deal of detail and use a literary style while others write very briefly and in note form.

The entries below and on page 60 are from four different diaries. Read them and then work through the activity on page 61.

A

Saturday, 18 April 1992

Dear Mimmy,
    There's shooting, shells are falling. This really is WAR. Mummy and Daddy are worried, they sit up until late at night, talking. They're wondering what to do, but it's hard to know. Whether to leave and split up, or stay here together. Keka wants to take me to Ohrid. Mummy can't make up her mind – she's constantly in tears. She tries to hide it from me, but I see everything. I see that things aren't good here. There's no peace. War has suddenly entered our town, our homes, our thoughts, our lives. It's terrible.
    It's also terrible that Mummy has packed my suitcase.

Love,
Zlata

B

Sunday, December 7th

Yesterday's wet clothes have dried on me, they're stuck to my skin. I'm giving up. Can't even be bothered now to crawl into the street.

I think it's Sunday, but what difference! Every day down at this level is Gloomday.

My mind is just a blank.

Each day here on skid row your mind and body take a beating and slowly but surely you become punch drunk.

Life is a survival course, you're forever searching for warmth and shelter only to be moved on.

All my worldly possessions are in a series of carrier bags. The handles constantly break, scattering everything I have all over the pavements.

C

DAY 70
3 DECEMBER

Sometime in the night we must have passed through Cleveland and Buffalo and Rochester on the southern shore of Lake Ontario. We're in New York State, heading due east along the gap in the Appalachian Mountains formed by the Mohawk River. The map is studded with classical names – Ithaca, Utica, Seneca Falls, Rome and Syracuse, the city we're drawing into as Nigel and I, the non-meatless, dig into eggs and bacon and that strange, burnt and watery substance that passes in America for coffee. Sitting across from us is a distinguished elderly man. He turns out to be 90 years old, an ex-air force commander called Skeel, who has traced back his Danish ancestors to the year A.D. 800 when they left Denmark and settled in East Anglia.

D

Friday July 23rd

11 am   A dirty white cat turned up on our doorstep this morning. It had a tag round its neck which said, 'My name is Roy' but there was no address. It ignored me when I got the milk in so I ignored it back.

6pm   My mother and father have had a big row about Roy. My father accused my mother of encouraging Roy to stay by giving him (the cat) a saucer of milk. My mother accused my father of being an animal hater.

The dog looks a bit worried; I expect it feels insecure. Roy spent the day asleep on the toolshed roof, unaware of the trouble it was causing.

Activities

Read through the four diary extracts on pages 59–60.

1   With a partner, discuss and then write down your ideas about:
    - *where* each diary was written – try to be as specific as possible
    - *what kind of person* wrote each extract (think about *age* and *gender*)
    - *the purpose* of the extract – why it was written
    - the writer's *intended audience*
    - *the tone* adopted by each writer.

2   Which of the extracts do you think are taken from a real diary? Which do you think are taken from a fictional diary? How easy or difficult is it to tell?

Audience and purpose

Diary entries can record trivial, everyday events which concern only one person, like the example below.

Simon's Diary March 12th 1997

Birthday today and woke up really early, excited. I thought about waking mum up but then thought that would be a bad idea. I thought again and decided that I couldn't wait any longer. Opened up all my cards and presents. Then got ready for school like the usual weekday morning routine. School was boring again apart from getting loads of cards and pressies and getting embarrassed in science when everyone sang happy birthday to me.

Diaries can also be written for a wider audience to record events on a national or international scale.

Samuel Pepys (1633–1703) kept a very famous diary which gave a detailed account of life in seventeenth-century London. The entries on page 62 were written in August 1665, at the time of an outbreak of bubonic plague in England. Read them and then answer the questions that follow them.

12th The people die so, that now it seems they are fain to carry the dead to be buried by day-light, the nights not sufficing to do it in. And my Lord Mayor commands people to be within at nine at night all, as they say, that the sick may have liberty to go abroad for ayre. There is one also dead out of one of our ships at Deptford, which troubles us mightily; the Providence, fire-ship, which was just fitted to go to sea. But they tell me to-day no more sick on board. And this day W Bodham tells me that one is dead at Woolwich, not far from the Rope-yard. I am told, too, that a wife of one of the groomes at Court is dead at Salisbury; so that the King and Queen are speedily to be all gone to Milton. So God preserve us!

15th It was dark before I could get home, and so land at Churchyard stairs, where, to my great trouble, I met a dead corps of the plague, in the narrow ally just bringing down a little pair of stairs. But I thank God I was so much disturbed at it. However, I shall beware of being late abroad again.

Questions

What information does Pepy's Diary give us about:

- how the authorities dealt with the epidemic
- what living conditions were like for ordinary people, and what they were like for the King and Queen
- Samuel Pepys?

Diary entries can also be used in fiction to give the audience more information about a character. This information is given not only by what the character writes (**direct information**), but also by the way the entry is written (**indirect information**).

Activities

The report below is from the novel *Flowers for Algernon*, by Daniel Keyes. Charlie Gordon is taking part in an experiment into human intelligence. He writes a daily diary in the form of a progress report. Read it, and then work through the activities below.

---

progris riport 1 martch 3

Dr Strauss says I shoud rite down what I think and remembir and evrey thing that happins to me from now on. I dont no why but he says its importint so they will see if they can use me. I hope they use me becaus Miss Kinnian says mabye they can make me smart. I want to be smart. My name is Charlie Gordon I werk in Donners bakery where Mr Donner gives me 11 dollers a week and bred or cake if I want. I am 32 yeres old and next munth is my brithday. I tolld dr Strauss and perfesser Nemur I cant rite good but he says it dont matter he says I shud rite just like I talk and like I rite compushishens in Miss Kinnians class at the beekmin collidge center for retarted adults where I go to lern 3 times a week on my time off. Dr. Strauss says to rite a lot evrything I think and evrything that happins to me but I cant think anymor because I have nothing to rite so I will close for today ... yrs truly Charlie Gordon.

‹WS40 **1** Although this is only the first page of the book, we gain a great deal of information about Charlie. Write down five **facts** that are given by Charlie in the report, for example:

> He works in Donner's bakery.

2 Now look in more detail at the way Charlie writes. Think about his:
- sentences and vocabulary
- paragraphs
- punctuation
- spelling.

Write down any mistakes that Charlie has made. Make a brief comment on each of these areas.

3 With a partner, compare your findings for questions **a** and **b**. What does this information tell you about Charlie?

This progress report is written by Charlie only three months after the first. Read it carefully, and then work through the activities below. As you read, think about the information you gained from the first entry.

PROGRESS REPORT 12

June 5 – Nemur is upset because I haven't turned in any progress reports in almost two weeks (and he's justified because the Welburg Foundation has begun paying me a salary out of the grant so that I won't have to look for a job). The International Psychological Convention at Chicago is only a week away. He wants his preliminary report to be as full as possible, since Algernon and I are the prime exhibits for his presentation.

Our relationship is becoming increasingly strained. I resent Nemur's constant references to me as a laboratory specimen. He makes me feel that before the experiment I was not really a human being.

I told Strauss that I was too involved in thinking, reading, and digging into myself, trying to understand who and what I am, and that writing was such a slow process it made me impatient to get my ideas down. I followed his suggestion that I learn to type, and now that I can type nearly seventy-five words a minute, it's easier to get it all down on paper.

WS41 4 Compare the way Charlie writes in June with the way he wrote in his first progress report, looking again at his:

- sentences and vocabulary
- paragraphs
- punctuation
- spelling.

Comment briefly on the changes in each area. What does this information suggest is happening to Charlie?

WS42 5 Professor Nemur and Doctor Strauss are mentioned in both entries

- Who do you think these people are?
- What does Charlie think of them?
- Does Charlie's opinion of them change from March to June?

Write down your thoughts, remembering to use quotes from the text to back up the points you make.

6 The second report does not say anything **directly** about the progress of the experiment but there is a great deal of **indirect information** which gives you clues. Discuss your findings, from **a** and **b** above, with a partner and say what you think has happened and how successful the experiment has been.

7 Now choose a fictional character – it could be someone from a book you have read or a character from a TV series, for example. Write two diary entries which give both direct and indirect information to your audience about the character.

Unit summary

In this unit you have learned:

- Diaries can be written for a range of purposes.
- Diaries are often written like informal letters and do not have strict rules of presentation.
- Diaries can be written for the writer alone, or for a much larger audience.
- In fiction, diaries can provide a lot of information about a character.

Activity

Write two diary entries. The first should detail everyday events in your life and is not meant to be read by anyone else; the second should deal with current national or international issues, and may become a historical document. Think about the different style and tone you will use for the two entries.

A6 Explanation and instruction

This unit will look at writing which gives information through **explanation** and **instruction**. This type of writing may tell you:

- how to do something
- how to get somewhere
- how something works
- what something looks like
- what you need to do.

Written information can be presented in many different forms, including leaflets, posters, letters, newspapers and magazines. New ways of communicating information, such as teletext, the Internet and e-mails, continue to develop.

Audience and purpose

As in all writing, the language you use and the tone you adopt will depend on your intended *audience* and *purpose* – who you are writing for, and why. Some explanations and instructions will require a colloquial, informal tone, while others are better suited to a more formal style. For example, a leaflet written for primary school children, on safety in the playground, will obviously be less complex and contain simpler language than an information sheet about the dangers of substance abuse, aimed at a teenage audience.

 Note

Whoever your audience and whatever your purpose, you will have to make your writing clear and think carefully about:

- **how you are going to present the information** (as a leaflet ... as a poster ... as a newspaper or magazine article ...)
- **how much information to include** (too much information may confuse the reader)
- **the balance between fact and opinion** (remember your main purpose is to inform, not to persuade)
- **your choice of language** (make sure that you explain any technical terms, unless you know that your audience will already be aware of them)
- **the visual impact** (how will you make your finished text look attractive and appealing to the reader?).

Similarities and differences

There are many similarities between explanations and instructions. The boxes below show some of their similarities and differences.

Explanations

- each piece of information is carefully sequenced and developed
- generally longer, more complex sentences
- sub-headings can be used
- factual descriptions
- reader not addressed directly – passive voice often used
- technical terms defined.

Example: *how to boil an egg*.

An egg can be boiled by placing it in a pan, half-filled with cold water. The pan is then placed on a source of heat and the heat is turned on. The water is boiled for four minutes (a timer should be used to help in this process). When four minutes have elapsed, the pan is removed from the heat and the egg is taken from the pan with a spoon. Finally, the egg is placed in an egg-cup.

Instructions

- very ordered structure – clear and simple
- short, simple sentences often in note form
- sometimes numbered (but not always!)
- factual descriptions
- directives/commands used – address readers directly and tell them what to do.

Example: *how to boil an egg*.

1 Half-fill a pan with cold water.
2 Place egg in pan.
3 Put pan on heat source.
4 Turn heat on.
5 When water starts to boil, start timing.
6 After four minutes, remove pan from heat.
7 Remove egg from pan with a spoon.
8 Place egg in egg-cup.

Activity

Study the information above, and then write a set of instructions and an explanation for each of the following:

- how to make a cheese sandwich
- how to record your favourite TV programme.

Presentational devices

The presentation of a text, especially in a leaflet, poster or advice sheet can help to attract and maintain a reader's attention. You should consider using some or all of the following when you write to instruct or explain:

Headings should stand out and grab the reader's attention. They may be bigger than the words in the main part of the text, or they may be in **bold type** or in a different colour or in CAPITAL LETTERS

Caption to highlight what is shown in the photograph, diagram or illustration

Sub-headings serve a similar purpose to headings; they help to break up the text and summarize what information is in the following text

Paragraphs are often relatively short, interesting and to the point

Photographs, diagrams and illustrations add variety and give the reader's eyes a rest from reading the text. They are often clearer and easier to understand than a written explanation

Bold type/colour– again, putting important or key words or phrases into bold type or in a different colour highlights those words

Bullet points help to break up the text and draw attention to key points

TACTICS AND TEAMWORK — GROUP 2 / CARD 29

Short passing

Good footballing sides always play a short passing game. It demands patience, great technique, constant movement off the ball and good communication plus, more importantly, excellent ball control.

A good short pass is one that allows the receiver to control the ball effortlessly. This usually means playing to feet rather than into space, keeping the ball on the ground and making sure the pass is weighted correctly.

Making space

Short passing is not just about keeping possession of the ball for its own sake. The short pass is very effective in creating space for other players to run into. If two or three players are playing keep-ball using short passes, defenders can lose patience and dive in to the tackle, leaving gaps in their defence.

Players with the confidence to play a close-passing game can usually spot the chance to release a sudden defence-splitting pass, which can then lead to a shot at goal.

David Beckham makes it look easy – playing a short pass out to the right wing

Use the side of your foot for maximum accuracy

Short and sharp

Skills check
- Good first touch and control
- Skilful side-foot technique
- Constant movement off the ball
- Good communication

Coach says
- Be quick, but be accurate.
- Your body language can signal your intentions – don't 'telegraph' where and when you intend to pass.
- Don't pass if it gets a team-mate into trouble.

Or video 3

Tactics in action Liverpool – the pass masters

Liverpool are shown as one of the best passing sides in the Premiership. Their short game is very effective – particularly when midfielders McManaman, Ince and Redknapp are involved. Liverpool's patient build-ups lull defenders into a false sense of security; and then suddenly a telling pass is made into space – usually for strikers like Robbie Fowler to run on to and shoot for goal. Midfielders with accuracy and a good first touch, such as Jamie Redknapp, are at the hub of such a movement; they can contribute several passes before the decisive ball is played.

Jamie Redknapp looks forward, ready to pass to a Liverpool team-mate.

Soccer Brilliance

Activities

Study the two advertisements below, which give information about the services offered by the National Express coach company. The first is taken from a local telephone directory, the second from the guide to the 1999 Glastonbury Festival.

1   Make a list of the differences between the two advertisements. Look particularly at the presentational devices and the language used.

2   Why are they different? (Think about the intended audience of each advertisement.)

3   Which advertisement do you prefer, and why?

A

B

A closer look

Activities

Look at the following extracts. For each one, decide whether it is instructing or explaining and then think about the audience for which it is written, its purpose and what kind of text it came from.

A

When's the best time to stop?

When's the best time to stop? You've thought about it, you've talked about it. Perhaps you've even made several attempts at it. But if you're serious about stopping smoking, there's only one thing to do – and that's DO IT! It's a fact of life that the longer you put off your decision to stop, the more likely it is that you never will. Why waste more time? The information and advice on the following pages will tell you how to wean yourself off the tobacco habit, and most importantly how you can help yourself stay a successful ex-smoker …

Did you know …
Smoking 20 cigarettes a day over an average lifetime will cost you about £100,000 (allowing for inflation).

B

By car – Leave M1 at Junction 36, and follow the brown 'Elsecar Heritage' signs, taking the A6135 for approx. 2 miles. Turn left onto Broad Carr Road for 3/4 mile, then right onto Armroyd Lane, and right on Fitzwilliam Street. Free visitor car parking is available on Wentworth Road off the junction of Fitzwilliam Street and Wath Road.

C

English Test

Paper 2
Shakespeare play

Please read this page, but do not open the booklet until your teacher tells you to start. Write your name and school on the front cover of your answer booklet. If you have been given a pupil number, write that also.

D

leaving zilch behind

Greener Glastonbury has banned the use of polystyrene. Paper cups can be re-pulped or composted if they are cleaned off before being placed into the special containers and cans recycled.

Help the Litter Crew keep the festival litter-free by collecting rubbish around your camp-site and using the appropriate bags. Bin bags are freely available from Information Points.

Don't burn plastic.

The River Whitelake flows through this beautiful farm, into which all the ditches and streams drain. It's a lovely little river which teems with wildlife, all too easily poisoned, so please only use the provided loos and washing sites. Think of the gentle cows returning to graze and of the emerging badgers – imagine it to be your backyard and your dining table.

Do your bit, in the right place.

E

Play continues in a clockwise direction.

The next player has to place tiles on the board, across or down, to make a new word.

These tiles must join on to, or cross, those already on the board.

The tiles must always form complete words.

They must also make complete words with any tiles they are next to in adjacent rows.

Example:

Turn 1

Score:
'dog' $\boxed{1}$ + $\boxed{1}$ = 2

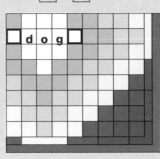

(taken from the 'Junior Scrabble' leaflet)

 1 Copy out and complete the table below and then, for each of the extracts above, state whether it is instructing or explaining, who the audience is, what its purpose is and what kind of text it comes from.

Extract	Explain/ Instruct	Audience	Purpose	Source
A				
B			Give directions	
C		fourteen year-old pupils		
D	E			
E				Leaflet

2 Choose one extract and explain how you worked out the answers to question 1. Use evidence from the text to support your answer.

Activities

 1 Look again at the bullet points in the Note box on page 66. Use them to help you to plan a short information leaflet or poster entitled 'How to get more pocket money from parents'. The leaflet/poster is aimed at the 11–14 age group and your purpose is to provide your audience with practical ideas.

2 Now try to create the leaflet or poster you have just planned. You have looked at a number of instructions and explanations in a number of different styles: pick out one or two which would be particularly suitable for your leaflet. Use presentational devices to make the finished product eye-catching and effective.

The extract below is taken from a Government pamphlet called 'A Highway Code for Young Road Users.' Study it carefully.

A HIGHWAY CODE FOR YOUNG ROAD USERS

Walking

When walking

1 Where there is a pavement or footway, walk on it. Keep as far away from traffic as possible.

2 Where there is no pavement, walk on the right hand side of the road to face the traffic coming towards you. Walk one behind the other at bends in the road or at night or if there is a lot of traffic. Take special care at right hand bends.

3 If you are looking after somebody younger than you, always hold their hand when using the road.

Be Safe, Be Seen

4 It is difficult for a driver to see you in the dark or in bad weather. When you have to be out then, always wear light-coloured or bright clothing. **Fluorescent** materials show up in daylight and at dusk. Always wear or carry something **reflective** at night.

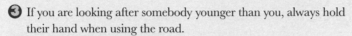

never run into the road ...

Questions

1 What presentational devices are used in this extract?
2 What do you notice about the language used in the extract?
3 What age range do you think the pamphlet is aimed at?
4 What is its purpose?

Activity

WS45 The next page of this leaflet, is titled 'How to Cross a Road Safely'. Write the next page in the style of the original, thinking particularly about your intended audience and purpose.

Unit summary

In this unit you have learned:

- Explanations and instructions are both useful ways of communicating information.
- When writing explanations and instructions, you must think carefully about your intended **audience** and the **purpose** of the writing.
- **Language** and **tone** are important considerations.
- **Presentational devices** can add to the appeal and impact of explanations and instructions.

Activity

Choose one task from each of the boxes below:

Writing to instruct

- Create a poster for a teenage audience, giving instructions on how to e-mail a message to a friend in the USA.

- Write out the instructions for your favourite recipe for a friend who has requested it.

- You are going on holiday and leaving your pet with a neighbour. Write out the instructions on how to feed your pet.

Writing to explain

- Write an explanation of the rules (or some of them) of your favourite sport or game, to a friend of the same age as you.

- Write a letter to your teacher explaining why you need an extra week to complete an English assignment.

- Create a leaflet for a teenage audience explaining how best to revise for the SATs exams.

Reports

What is a report?

What springs to mind when you think of a report? A newspaper report? Your school report? A Government report?

The word 'report' covers a wide range of writing. *The Collins Shorter English Dictionary* defines it as:

> *An account of an event, a situation, or a person's progress.*

Questions

The openings to five different types of report are given below.

- **Where** might you find these pieces of writing?
- **Who** is the audience for each piece of writing?

A

When the fire broke out, I telephoned my neighbour, and warned her about the fire.

Then I ran to my children's bedroom and ushered them downstairs as quickly as I could.

When I got outside, my neighbour was already standing in the street. The fire brigade arrived within two minutes.

B

Squirrels Close School

A Birmingham school was closed yesterday, when it was discovered that the attic floor of the building was infested with squirrels.

The discovery was made when a small grey squirrel landed on the head of 12-year-old Michael Jones while he was in his Science lesson at Kilby Road Secondary School.

C

We are now progressing well in the project. Jane has completed the art work, and Meera and Sam have written the articles ready for publication. Peter has contacted two companies.

D

Last week, we had our Year 8 disco in the main hall at school. Over two hundred people enjoyed the event. Thanks go to 'Light 'n' Sound' for providing the music and lights.

E

Last year, in terms of work and behaviour, Matthew hit rock bottom. This year, he's started drilling.

Audience

Before writing a report it is important to know who the audience is. Is it a national television audience? Is the audience the general public of a particular town or village? Is it young people, or retired people? Is your audience one person who wants to read an account of an incident at school?

You should always adjust your writing according to your audience.

Questions

1. If the passage below appeared in a report for a national newspaper, what additional information would you expect to find in it?

> Last night, Mr Eric Johnson was hurt when a tree fell on his car. Mr Johnson went to Kilby Hospital, and is said to be shocked but happy to be alive.
>
> The car was parked in Wellsop Road. Inspector Blakeford said that he had never seen anything like it in twenty years as a serving police officer.

2. **a** If the passage below appeared in a school magazine, who would your audience be?
   b Bearing that in mind, what information could be missed out? Why?

> **Last month, class 7E of Kilby High School, Northants, was lucky enough to visit the Globe Television Studios, in Upper Perditon, Surrey.**
>
> The class was accompanied by Mr Ronald Evans (48), who has been at Kilby School for eighteen years. He has been Head of the Media Studies Department since 1994.
>
> While they were at the studios, the pupils operated cameras, sat at the director's desk, read the news and even acted on the set of the Globe's most famous soap, *West Street*.
>
> Mr Evans said that the trip was a great success. He was particularly pleased with student Rajinder Kaur (11), of Newlands Road, Kilby, who wrote and directed a scene for *West Street*.

Starting a report

The **opening section** of a report is very important: after reading this, the reader should have a pretty good idea what the rest of the report is about.

Therefore, the opening section of a report should *always* answer these three questions:

- **What?** what has happened, what is the situation, what progress has been made, etc.

- **Who?** who is or was involved.

- **When?** when the event took place, progress made over how long, etc.

In addition, reports on *events* should also answer a fourth question:

- **Where?** where the event took place.

Activity

WS47

Read the six openings below and on page 77. Do they answer the **What? Who? When?** and **Where?** questions? In a table like the one on page 77, identify which openings answer the questions and which do not.

A

Yesterday evening, six people were injured in a road accident when a lorry and a car collided on the busy A132 near Kilby.

B

I have seen his fitness improve greatly, in terms of both speed and stamina.

C

On the night in question, Tuesday 16th March, I was walking home along Boothferry Road when I witnessed two men breaking into the computer shop.

D

Two gangs of youths fought each other with glass bottles and iron bars. It was a violent incident, and police have arrested seven people.

E

In our group there are currently four people: James, Levi, Tamin and Natalie. We have been working together since September.

F

Peter has made very good progress in his reading in the last six months.

Opening	What?	Who?	When?	Where?
A	People were injured when a lorry collided with a car	Six people		
B				
C				
D				
E				
F				

Developing a report

Having looked at what makes a good opening to a report, it is important to know how to develop it.

Look again at the opening to report A, and then look at the way it has been developed below.

Yesterday evening, six people were injured in a road accident when a lorry and a car collided on the busy A132 near Kilby.

This opening answers all four questions:

- **What?**
- **Who?**
- **When?**
- **Where?**

The lorry driver, a 42-year-old man, was taken to Kilby General Hospital but was later discharged with mild concussion. The other five people, who were all in the car, were also taken to the hospital. Car driver Kevin Preston (33), and his front-seat passenger Ann Taylor (35), were detained with injuries described by Dr Jane Bradley as serious but not life-threatening. The three rear-seat passengers have since been discharged with minor injuries.

This paragraph goes on to give more **details** about the crash. The reader is told about:

- The people who were involved
- their injuries.

Notice also that the *opinion* of the hospital doctor is included here. Her opinion is written in **reported speech**. You will often see reported speech in news reports.

Note

Reported speech differs from **direct speech** because the actual words spoken are *not* used. Therefore, you do *not* use **speech marks** with reported speech.

Police believe that icy road conditions were the main cause of the accident. This theory was confirmed by Kilby resident Mavis Jacobs, who lives near the A132. She was walking her dog at the time of the accident and told our reporter: 'I saw the lorry approach the bend quite slowly, but then it seemed to hit a patch of ice and slid across the road into the oncoming car.'

This section starts to consider the questions **How?** and **Why?**
- **How** did the accident happen?
- **Why** did the accident happen?

In suggesting reasons for this the newspaper reporter quotes an onlooker – someone who was an **eyewitness** to the accident.

In the previous section, the reporter used **reported speech**. Here, to vary things a little, **direct speech** is used.

Note

When using **direct speech**, you *do* need to use **speech marks**.

Both vehicles then left the carriageway, and ploughed through a hedge before coming to rest in a field of nearby Bycroft Farm.

This paragraph reveals **more details** of the accident.

Police Constable Martin Jones was the first to arrive at the scene of the accident. He had been on duty on the Kingsley Estate when he heard the collision. 'I just ran immediately to the main road and was horrified when I saw what had happened,' he said.

In the next paragraph, another eyewitness is introduced.

Once again, the reporter has used **direct speech** so he has enclosed the actual words of the eyewitness in **speech marks**.

Police investigating the incident are still appealing for any other witnesses to the accident to come forward. They can telephone the police on 01629 433433.

Finally, the report finishes with an appeal for help from the public. However, it could have ended with alternatives like:

- a comment about the next steps in the investigation
- a comment on the number of recent accidents on this stretch of road
- a comment on the number of people who were injured due to icy road conditions on that particular night.

Activities

1   In this report, there are two pieces of reported speech, and two pieces of direct speech. Put the reported speech into direct form, and the direct speech into reported form. For example, the first will begin:

Dr Jane Bradley said today, 'The injuries ...'

2   Write a paragraph for each of the three alternative endings to the report that are suggested in the last box on this page. If you can think of some other alternative endings, write them out as well.

Activity

These two drafts of a report, below and on page 81, were both written for a school magazine, *Kilby High School News*. Read through **both** of the drafts, then complete the task below.

Note down all the improvements that have been made in the second draft. You could make your notes under the following headings:

- Headline
- Opening paragraph
- Details
  - which details have been included from the first draft?
  - which details have been missed out? Why?
  - which details have been moved? Why?
- Use of illustrations – what effect does this have?
- Use of direct and reported speech
- Ending

New Sports Hall Opened

The new sports hall was opened yesterday. People started arriving at three o'clock, and soon the car park was crowded with visitors.

A lot of chairs had been put in the sports hall by pupils in 8C for people to sit on, and gradually the hall filled with people. There was a hum of people talking excitedly to one another and after about fifteen minutes the headteacher went to the front of the room. He was wearing a dark suit and red checked tie. He took out his notes and put them on the stand and then he put his hands on each side of the stand and leaned forward slightly, standing on his toes a bit.

He said, 'I would like to welcome you all to Kilby High School today, for this very important day in our brief history.' His hands fumbled with the paper that he held in his hand. 'For today we are very proud to be opening our new sports hall. You only need to look around you to see how splendid it is. It will enable us to offer a wide range of sports to our youngsters.'

The sports hall had cost over a million pounds to build, and would enable students to take part in netball, basketball, five-a-side football, badminton, indoor hockey and many other sports.

Some of the money had been provided by the National Lottery Fund, some had been provided by the education authority, and some by sponsored events in the school. It certainly looked really nice.

Then footballer Andy Flynn got up. He used to attend the school. He said about how much he had enjoyed school, and then he cut the tape.

When he finished, we listened to the school band playing 'Football's Coming Home' and watched a display of sports skills by some of the boys and girls in year 10 and year 11.

Afterwards, everyone went home.

Footballer Andy Flynn Opens New Sports Hall

Andy Flynn, current Kilby Town captain and former pupil of Kilby High School, yesterday opened the new sports hall at a ceremony attended by over two hundred guests.

Andy, who attended Kilby High from 1983 to 1988, remarked on how happy he had been at the school, and how the school had taught him some lessons in life that he carried with him even today. He then cut the tape to mark the official opening of the hall, amid applause and cheers from all guests.

Earlier, headteacher Gordon Miller, who has himself been at Kilby High for seventeen years, the last eight as headteacher, had spoken of the opening being an important day in the history of the school. He told us that he was particularly pleased with the range of sports that the school would now be able to offer its youngsters, including netball, basketball, five-a-side football and indoor hockey.

The sports hall has cost over one million pounds to build. Much of the money was donated following an appeal to the National Lottery Fund, and the education authority had added what Mr Miller described as 'a significant sum'. The rest of the cash had been raised by the combined efforts of staff, pupils and parents in organizing a host of sponsored events.

The hall is over sixty metres in length, and is therefore one of the largest school sports halls in the country. In all, over ten thousand floor tiles were laid, nearly sixty tins of paint were used, and the heating and lighting for the building demanded over two miles of electrical cabling!

We at the Kilby High School News would like to thank everyone for their wonderful efforts in providing this outstanding facility for the pupils of the school.

At the end of the ceremony, the school band played a rousing chorus of the football anthem 'Football's Coming Home'. Perhaps more appropriately, sport is coming home – to Kilby High School.

Activity

This page contains notes made on a school drama production, called *Ghostly Laughter*. Page 83 contains notes on a cup final which was won by Kilby School's team.

Write two reports for the school magazine, based on these notes. You can add any further details that you like to make the reports really 'authentic'.

You will need to reorganize your cup final notes quite a lot!

Ghostly Laughter

- Comedy set in an old castle.

- Performed for three nights – sold out of tickets every night. December 10th – 12th.

- Cast of ten people. Over twenty working behind the scenes – stage manager, make-up, costumes, lighting, sound, set design, set creation, etc.

- Great set designed by Mr Cole, Head of Technology – full of secret panels and other surprises.

- Sam Whitman was brilliant as the ancient butler, Gripe. A sniggering old man. (Excellent make-up – pasty face, blackened teeth.)

- Julie Worsley also very talented – star of the future – as Lisa, a clever circus girl who traps an escaped convict.

- Leading role taken by Jason Howell – in the sixth form – bumbling old husband. Very funny performance.

- Director – Mrs Mason. 'I'm really proud of the boys and girls who took part. They were marvellous.'

- Headteacher – Miss Hughes. 'This just shows everybody what can be done when people work together. A magnificent achievement.'

Cup Final

- Cup Final between Kilby School Senior Football Team and Weston School Senior Football Team

- At Kilby School on Saturday May 5th

FIRST HALf

- Kilby first to attack – Mark Johnson shot over the bar – good pass from Paul Jacobs – 6 mins

- Weston hit post – 30 yards – James Tallent (striker who is on the books of Derby County) – 11 mins

- Weston player booked for arguing with referee – 24 mins

- Weston open scoring – header from Tallent – 31 mins

- 2nd Weston goal – clever run by Raj Sund through Kilby defence – 34 mins

- Kilby attack – Matthew Richards misses from six yards – 42 mins.

SECOND HALF

- Kilby score – Richards slid ball in from Murray's cross – 48 mins

- James Tallent misses opportunity to make it 3-1 – 65 mins

- Kilby equalize – Tran Hong header at near post – cross by Richards – 86 mins

- Kilby score winner – shot from Matthew Richards – 89 mins.

Writing a report of a situation

On page 74, the definition of a report was given as:

An account of an event, a situation, or a person's progress.

In this section you will learn how to write a report on a *situation*.

The situation that you will be reporting on is a real one, from the middle of the nineteenth century when children were often forced to work from the age of seven or eight.

In 1844, Mr Samuel Scriven, a Government inspector, interviewed over a hundred children who worked in and around Stoke-on-Trent. He was trying to find out what their working conditions were like. He asked each of them to describe their working day.

The notes that he made on six of those children are printed on this page and the next. After making his notes, Samuel Scriven had to write a report for the Government called 'The working conditions of children in the Potteries' (Stoke-on-Trent and the surrounding area).

Read the notes he made and then work through the Activities on page 86.

Susan Wilcox, aged 10

I am an apprentice burnisher to Mr Allcock. I polish dishes before they are sent out. I have been there for twelve months. There are three apprentices, and thirty or forty women working in the same room with me. There are three superintendents looking over us. Sometimes they
5 give me a slap on the back when I look off my work. That is all the punishment I get, except a scolding. I get rewarded sometimes with a penny, when I'm a good girl. The burnishers give it, not the master. I get one shilling six pence a week and carry it home to mother. I can read and write a bit. I go to Sunday School, and went to a day school afore I came.

James Badley, aged 12

I am a runner of moulds for Frederick Barnet: I carry the hot moulds out of the kilns. I can read and write. I went to day school in Cobridge before I came to work. I come at six o'clock, and go home at eight, and I have three shillings a week. Frederick Barnet pays me regular. He sometimes
5 gives me a penny if I'm a good lad. If I'm a bad one, he lays on me. He never struck me more than once; he didn't hurt me much. My father is a dish maker; my mother a painter of plates. I like my work pretty well. I do not go home to breakfast. I am allowed half an hour. Master allows us an hour for dinner. I only have half of it, and then I have to work again.
10 When I come in the morning, I am here first and get the fire in.

Josiah Wilkinson, aged 11

I make the clay for William Bentley. I have been at work for five years. I cannot read or write; never went to day school. I get three shillings and six pence a week. I come at half past six to work, and go home at nine; work Mondays and every day. William Bentley licks me with his fist. He
5   has knocked me the other side of the pot stove for being so long at breakfast. Half an hour is allowed, but he makes me work before the half hour is up. I go home to dinner, but he won't let me bide an hour. I live a quarter of a mile away, and have to run home and back out of it. I never get a bit of play. I'm very tired when get home at night; get my supper
10 and am glad to go to bed. I get a bit of meat for breakfast, and taters and salt for dinner, and sometimes a bit of bacon. I would rather work 10 hours a day than 15. I should not care if I had less wages a good sight. I should go to school then, and have a bit of time for play.

Mary Ann Bailey, aged 12

I have been apprenticed to Mr Wood for two years as a paper cutter. We make stencils for the people who paint the saucers. I cannot read or write; I never went to day school since I was a little girl. I do not
5   go to Sunday School, as mother is ill. I come to work at seven and leave at five. In our room there are sixteen girls working with me. Six of them cannot read their names; nine of the whole sixteen can write. I get bread and cheese and coffee for
10 breakfast, and pork-pie for dinner; sometimes meat and tatees. I always get enough. I like my work very much, and my mistress is very good to me. I never get punished except by getting another piece or two to do if we do not behave. If we are good girls we give over
15 sooner than usual.

Hannah Lowton, aged 6

I make cockspurs for Mr Holland, which means I make up fires and sweep the floors. I don't know how long I have been to work. Mother is here too; father is dead. I can read, but I cannot write. I went to day school. I don't go to Sunday School. I get one shilling a week. I come
5   sometimes at six o'clock, and sometimes after. I go home when mother does at nine o'clock. I've got a brother and a sister. One makes cockspurs, and the other runs moulds. I like to come to work. Father died of cough. They called it decline.

Activities

1   Record the information you are given in the children's statements in a table like the one below. Where you have no information, leave the box blank.

Name	Age	Age when started work	Type of work	Hours	Pay	Rewards and punishments	Education
Susan Wilcox							
James Badley							
Josiah Wilkinson							
Mary Ann Bailey							
Hannah Lowton							

Sometimes, when writing a report, you will want to **summarize** information. For example, if you conducted a survey on the time that people in your class go to bed, you would not give the whole list of responses when you report your results. You would summarize the information, like this:

Most people go to bed between 10.00 pm and 11.00 pm, though five pupils said that they go to bed after 11.00 pm, and two after midnight.

2   Imagine you are Mr Scriven. A local newspaper reporter interviews you about your survey. Use your completed table to help you to answer the questions below. Try to summarize the information that you have – the table should help you to do so.
   a   At what age do children tend to start work in the Potteries?
   b   How many hours a day do these children work?
   c   What type of work are they expected to do?
   d   What are they paid for their work?
   e   How are they treated by adults in authority over them?
   f   Do these children go to school?

3   Now imagine you are the reporter. Write up your notes in the form of an interview script. It has been started for you below.

Reporter   At what age do children tend to start work in the Potteries?

Mr Scriven   It varies, of course, but I would say that on average, children are about eight or nine years old. However, sometimes children as young as six are working.

Mr Scriven also interviewed many adults about the employment of children in the Potteries. One of their accounts is printed on this page and one on page 88.

George Ryles, Inspector of Police

I have lived all my life in Burslem; was born in it. The nature of my occupation was that of printer, and later, that of police officer. I am well acquainted with the practices of workmen and with the employment of children.

Some little girls from nine years of age come to work at six in the morning, and occasionally at four or five. They first begin by making up the fire and cleaning up the shop. They get coals for the day, and get out the ashes, broken ware and that sort of thing. Some of them fetch water for use of the room, and this is heavy work.

They are allowed half an hour for breakfast, and an hour for dinner, but seldom exceed forty minutes, and very often not fifteen. If the trade requires it, they work to seven, eight and sometimes nine o'clock at night.

Sometimes, they are sent out on errands. This occupies the time of the child who, on her return, has to fetch it up by hard labour. Often, she is rewarded by the printer with a flogging, blows, hard words or cursing.

Boys often come to work at five or half past. Whenever their masters have neglected their work in the early part of the week, they then have their boys at work at four, and I have known them begin at three. They are allowed half an hour for breakfast, and an hour for dinner. The masters require them invariably to work during meal times, and continue them up to eight or nine o'clock at night.

Some of these masters behave very cruelly to them. I have known repeated instances where masters come to work under the effects of drunkenness. When they want a relish, such as a red-herring, or something sharp, such as vinegar and ham, they send the children out to commit petty thefts in the marketplace, to gratify their appetites.

I'll give you an example. A child of nine or ten years of age was taken up for cutting off a water tap and lead pipe. I found that this child had been instructed by his master where to find it, and to bring it to him. He afterwards directed him where to dispose of it, and return to him with the proceeds of the sale. The child was committed for trial. At the trial, I stated to the chairman that I had reason to believe that the child was instructed by his master. The child was sentenced to three days' imprisonment. I afterwards ascertained that my suspicions, as it regards the master, were correct, but nothing was done with *him*

Robert Glass, workman at Mellor, Venables and Pinder Earthenware Factory, Burslem

I have been employed in the potting trade for 26 years come next June. Until the last two years, I was employed in what is technically called the *flat branch*, as dish, plate and saucer making, as a workman. I am a workman now in the china manufactory, which is much less laborious than earthenware.

I have always considered mould-running in earthenware very laborious. The mould-runner has to run to and fro from the jigger to the stove with generally two saucers at a time, and this *twice over*, first to lay on the ware, and then for the polishing. I consider the excessive heat which he has to labour in, and the steam which is constantly passing off from the work, to be very injurious to his health; although it does not produce deformities of the body, it nevertheless stunts growth, and produces premature death, asthma or consumption; very few men live beyond the age of 45.

In the dipping-houses, children are subject to injuries from the effects of the ingredients that are used in the glosses; but the proportion of children so employed are small.

The treatment of children in some rooms by young 'prentices is oftentimes rough, and sometimes brutal. It arises from their vulgar brutality – the want of proper education. The labour of young girls is moderate, but they are made to carry water from the yards upon their heads. I have often seen them overburdened.

I have known many cases where children are obliged to fetch liquor for the working men, and drink portions themselves. Before I became more reflective, I regret to say I revelled in the like sin!

They have been prompted to steal. I have known such cases where men are getting a hash, and wanted a few onions, and they have sent children to the market stalls to beg and, if refused, have been told to watch the opportunity to run off with a bunch. They are commonly told to lie.

There are a great many workmen who play on the Monday partially, and who work hard in the middle days. The boys work with them, and frequently continue for 15 hours a day. My opinion is that they should not be allowed to do so. I believe it would be better for children, and benefit the manufacturer, if he closed his gates at six o'clock.

I believe the children in the Potteries are below par in point of moral conduct, and I should say that this is a result of the ignorance of the adult population. To remedy this, it is necessary to establish a good system of moral education for the rising generation, by establishing institutions in which rational and healthful amusements and industrial training is observed and carried out.

Activities

1. After reading the statements of Inspector Ryles and Mr Glass, list the *new things* that we have learned, to add to the things that we already knew from the statements of the children. Some of their evidence expands on what the children said, but some is completely new.

2. Imagine you are Mr Scriven. Write your report for your boss.

   You should:

   - tell him briefly about your work (What? Who? When? Where?)
   - tell him what you have found out about the treatment of children in the Potteries
   - suggest some new regulations which would improve the children's living and working conditions.

Unit summary

In this unit you have learned:

- The start of the report should answer the questions:

  What?   (what has happened, or what the report is about)

  Who?   (who is involved)

  When?   (when the event happened, or the time period involved in a report of progress made on a project)

  Where?   (this, of course, only applies to a report of an **event**).

- The next part of the report should then give further details of each of the above and answer the questions **How?** and **Why?**
- In adding details, you can use **eyewitness accounts** and people's comments on an event or activity.
- Eyewitness accounts and people's comments can be expressed as **direct speech** or **reported speech**.

Activity

Make a set of notes about an event at your school – for example, a sports match, a musical or drama activity, a newly formed club or society, or a school trip. Then write up your notes as a report for your school's own magazine.

A8 Persuasive writing

There are many occasions in daily life when you see writing which tries to influence what you do or think. If you pick up a magazine, or watch television, you see a range of advertisements which are all trying to persuade you in some way – usually to buy something. Similarly, we all read articles in books, magazines or leaflets which try to change the way we think about a subject or topic.

This unit looks at how to identify the techniques used to persuade readers, and how to use them to write persuasively in different situations.

Audience and purpose

The two most important points to consider when writing to persuade are:

- **Audience** – who will be reading your writing?
- **Purpose** – your reason for writing it.

When you have decided upon your audience and purpose, you need to think carefully about the tone and language you will use to help get your message across.

The **tone** you adopt will depend upon your audience and purpose. You could, for example, decide to make your writing humorous as a way of getting your message across, or you could write in a much more serious tone.

Remember, you are trying to persuade your audience, so when you are considering the sort of **language** to use, think about including:

- **emotive words** which arouse strong feelings in the reader and encourage them to read on. For example:

> The **new** Ariston FM51R built-in oven is styled in Italy, with a **breathtaking** stainless steel and mirror glass finish

- **directive language** which gives instructions or orders. In this way, the readers feel as if you are speaking directly to them. For example:

> **Change** the face of your kitchen

- **rhetorical questions** – these are questions which are directed at the readers, but do not require answers. Again, the readers feel as if they are being spoken to directly. For example;

> In providing accommodation for over 1000 people a night, St Mungo's has set itself very high standards indeed. **Will you help us maintain those standards?**

You could also think about using one or more of the following approaches, to help persuade your readers:

Persuasive words or phrases

These will make your audience think that they should either agree with your point of view or else be seen as unreasonable. For example:

> *obviously, without a doubt, undeniably, surely, definitely, certainly ...*

Personal pronouns

When you use personal pronouns such as *we, us, you*, you are trying to involve the reader directly.

Informal language

Addressing your audience as if you know them, by using *informal* or *colloquial* language, can be an effective means of persuasion. Using language in this way gives a conversational tone to the writing and can make the reader regard you as a friend.

Repetition

If you say something just once, it can be easily forgotten so, if you have a certain message to get across, try to ensure that you say it more than once.

Presentational devices

Look back to page 68 of Unit 6, 'Explanation and instruction', for more details on presentational devices such as:

> *headings, sub-headings, paragraphs, bullet points, bold type, exclamation marks, photographs, diagrams and illustrations.*

Look at the adverts below. What techniques have been used to persuade their audience?

THE SS UNIVERSE EXPLORER

The *Universe Explorer* is unlike most of the vessels which cruise the Alaskan waters. Travelling with you will be a number of experts on the area who will provide talks and briefings on Alaska's history, culture, geology, natural history and botany, and, in addition, passengers have the benefit of a vast library.

Of course we do not forget that you are on holiday and everything you could possibly require is at hand ...

Fact or opinion?

It is important to be able to distinguish fact from opinion in what you read *and* in your own writing.

Facts are things that can be proved – they are true, and no one can contradict them. For example:

> *'Wannabe' was a hit for the Spice Girls.*

Opinions are more personal – they are what people think, and there can be a number of opinions on just one subject. For example:

> *The Spice Girls are the best group in the world.*

Activity

Look at the following extract from a car advertisement which gives details of a competition prize. Write down five facts and five opinions which appear in the extract. Is it the facts or the opinions that would persuade you to enter the competition? Why?

Chicago skyline

Win a wonderful holiday in Chicago – staying at the historic Ambassador West Hotel – the most elegant of 'Grand Heritage Hotels'

Established in 1924, The Ambassador West Hotel has been beautifully restored in the grand European manner and offers classic old-world charm and elegance. Beautiful and elegant décor, first-class service and a tradition of comfort.

With a special place in the hearts and minds of everyone who has ever stayed there, it is located in the heart of the Gold Coast, downtown Chicago's most affluent residential, shopping and business areas. Truly in the heart of Chicago's city life.

Take your time seeing the world-renowned Navy Pier, Oak Street Beach and Lincoln Park Zoo. Shop in the Magnificent Mile – and take full advantage of Chicago's nightlife.

The prize includes 7 nights at the hotel – on a bed and breakfast basis – before 15 December 1999 and is subject to availability.

The winner will fly from London. To make a reservation or to find out more about Grand Heritage Hotels please call 0171 244 6699.

Examining and writing persuasive material

Activities

1 Look at the following extracts and work out how each one attempts to persuade the reader. For each passage you should think about:
- the intended audience
- its purpose
- where you might find it
- how it tries to persuade you.

2 Which passage do you find the most effective?

A

Enjoy one of the most beautiful and romantic places in the world with 600 miles of unspoilt and uncrowded coastline, wild scenery and cool green mountains.

Villas with pools, cottages by the sea, medieval village houses, carefully selected hotels.

Let us help you plan that special holiday. Very friendly personal service. For brochure Tel: 01424 460046/fax460033

ATOL 2647 AITO

B

The new one-day contact lenses

simple ... and affordable

Convenient
No lens care

Comfortable
Unique ultra-thin edge

Healthy
Fresh new lenses every day

Affordable
So you can wear them every day

New! Focus DAILIES™
ONE-DAY CONTACT LENSES

FREE TRIAL OFFER¹ Focus DAILIES™
ONE-DAY CONTACT LENSES

C

A beautifully situated Cotswold stone house with mature gardens and grounds, enjoying outstanding and far-reaching views.

Activities

Read carefully through the information below. The basic information was obtained from a website on the Internet, and was originally in the form of a leaflet. However, it has been reorganized so that much of its persuasiveness has been left out.

WS59 Imagine that you work for WWF – World Wide Fund For Nature, which is working to save tigers from possible extinction. Your task is to use the information below to write a **persuasive** leaflet on this issue.

Your audience is Key Stage 3 secondary school pupils (ages 11–14).

1   First of all, think about what view (or views) you are putting forward; you will have to choose which pieces of information to use and which to leave out in support of these views.

2   Think carefully about the tone of your text.

3   Decide what kind of presentational devices to use.

There are some headings/sub-headings beneath the passage which you might like to use in your leaflet. Alternatively, you could create your own.

Tigers

There are only about 5000 tigers left in the world today.

Manau Pothi is a 9-year-old female Bengal tiger living in the Royal Bardia National Park in Nepal.

The park helps to keep the tigers safe from the threat of poachers.

Poachers outside the park want to kill the tigers to make money.

Poachers aren't the only things threatening Manau Pothi and other tigers.

In the last twenty years, more than one million hectares of forest have disappeared.

Much of the forest has been taken over by industrial buildings and land that people have cleared for farming.

This has meant that the tigers' food resources have shrunk.

The number of places in the forest where tigers used to live has also grown smaller.

WWF – World Wide Fund For Nature wants to stop the destruction of the forests and to save the tigers.

They are asking for people to adopt Manau Pothi for only £2 per month.

This helps protect her from poachers.

Donations like this help WWF equip and keep mobile anti-poaching patrols in the areas where the tigers are most at risk – in Asia and the Russian Far East.

They want to monitor the tigers to ensure they live and breed in a safe habitat.

WWF wants the tigers to live in their natural homes again.

People who adopt Manau Pothi will receive a certificate, a photograph of her and reports on her progress four times a year.

Possible headings/sub-headings

Adopt a tiger before it's too late

Help us to help the tigers

You can help stop the slaughter

Help us to fight the poachers

Activity

Look at the following advertisement by an estate agent, which appeared in a local newspaper.

This advertisement gives **information** about the house, but it also tries to **persuade** prospective buyers that this is the house for them. It has been labelled to show the main features which might help to do this.

Photographs chosen to show house in a positive light.

Headline in **bold** to catch your eye and make you want to read on. The emotive words 'with character' add interest to the description.

THREE BEDROOMED VICTORIAN SEMI WITH CHARACTER

This is a <u>most impressive</u> family home which has been <u>carefully</u> and <u>sympathetically</u> improved, retaining original character, <u>enhanced</u> by decorative features having stripped panelled doors, period fireplace and stained glass windows. You will enter by a vestibule entrance to the reception hall, <u>large elegant</u> dining room, <u>impressive</u> lounge, <u>spacious</u> breakfast room and split-level fitted kitchen. There are three <u>generous</u> bedrooms and a bathroom on the first floor. <u>Long</u> rear garden and off-road parking to the front. This <u>lovely</u> home is centrally heated and <u>very well presented</u>.

WHY NOT RING US TO ARRANGE A FULL INSPECTION SO YOU CAN APPRECIATE THIS <u>DELIGHTFUL</u> PROPERTY

Frequent use of the emotive words (underlined) to emphasize the good points of the house.

The **tone** is serious, but the **language** used is often very informal – as though the writing was addressed to a friend who had asked for the information.

Use of capital letters at the end – to summarize the information and to focus the reader's attention – a final 'plea' to arouse your interest.

Imagine that you are interested in buying this house. You visit the estate agent and are given the details about the house which are printed on the next page. Read them and then work through the questions that follow.

A MOST IMPRESSIVE CAREFULLY IMPROVED THREE BEDROOM VICTORIAN SEMI DETACHED RESIDENCE

The spacious accommodation comprises:

* IMPRESSIVE LOUNGE *

Having a stripped pine fire surround with cast insert and living-flame gas fire and a tiled hearth, original leaded stained glass side window, wide bay window with opening French windows leading to the rear garden area.

* SPACIOUS BREAKFAST ROOM *

A good sized family room with an original cast iron fireplace with tiled side panels, quarry tiled floor, double-glazed side bay window and stripped pine door to kitchen.

* MOST ATTRACTIVE SPLIT-LEVEL FITTED BREAKFAST KITCHEN *

Having a range of natural finish wood fronted units with contrasting marble effect work tops and having the original quarry tiled floor in the working kitchen area and a step down to stripped floor in lower level area with matching units and a wood panelled sloping ceiling. Plumbing for dishwasher, built in wine rack, corner cupboard and end shelving. One double and one single wall cupboard, integrated freezer and refrigerator, central work top with four-ring gas hob and oven. Plenty of space for breakfast table and chairs. Telephone point. Two double-glazed windows to the side and one to the rear make this kitchen extremely light and spacious.

* REAR GARDEN *

A very long garden with a large paved patio area with charming stone steps down to a lawn area with mature shrubs and trees. Pathway through shaped and well stocked flower borders, bushes and rockery. The garden is well fenced and not directly overlooked from the rear. Please note that to the far end of this very long rear garden area planning permission has been granted to build a small development of new homes.

* SITUATION *

The property is situated in this very popular and convenient location, a short walk away from the main shopping area. There are frequent public transport facilities and easy access to local schools, railway station, the M40 and the airport. The property is also convenient for the Rover Car Company.

Questions

1. Why is the house described as a 'residence' in the title?
2. Make a list of all the **emotive words** in the descriptions. Choose three of these and say why they have been used. Do you think they are effective?
3. Why has the word 'original' been used a number of times, to describe various features?
4. Look carefully at the description of the rear garden. Is there any information here which might worry you?
5. In the last section, 'Situation', there are a number of details which are used to show how conveniently situated the house is – make a list of these. Now, write out this section again, but this time using the same details in a negative way. You could begin:

> The property is situated in a very crowded location right next to the noisy and very busy main shopping area ...

Activities

In this passage from *David Copperfield* by Charles Dickens, the young David is taken by his nurse 'Peggotty' to visit her brother, Mr Peggotty, in Yarmouth. Mr Peggotty lives with his nephew (Ham) and niece (Little Em'ly) on the beach in a rather unusual dwelling.

Read the passage and then complete the tasks which follow.

'Yon's our house, Mas'r Davy!'

I looked in all directions, as far as I could stare over the wilderness, and away at the sea, and away at the river, but no house could *I* make out. There was a black barge, or some other
5   kind of superannuated boat, not far off, high and dry on the ground, with an iron funnel sticking out of it for a chimney and smoking very cosily; but nothing else in the way of a habitation that was visible to *me*.

'That's not it?' said I. 'That ship-looking thing?'
10   'That's it, Mas'r Davy,' returned Ham.

If it had been Aladdin's palace, roc's egg and all, I suppose I could not have been more charmed with the romantic idea of living in it. There was a delightful door cut in the side, and it was roofed in, and there were little windows in it; but the
15   wonderful charm of it was, that it was a real boat which had no doubt been upon the water hundreds of times, and which had never been intended to be lived in, on dry land. That was the captivation of it to me. If it had ever been meant to be lived in, I might have thought it small, or inconvenient, or lonely; but
20   never having been designed for any such use, it became a perfect abode.

It was beautifully clean inside, and as tidy as possible. There was a table, and a Dutch clock, and a chest of drawers, and on the chest of drawers there was a tea-tray with a painting on it
25   of a lady with a parasol, taking a walk with a military-looking child who was trundling a hoop. The tray was kept from

tumbling down, by a bible; and the tray, if it had tumbled down, would have smashed a quantity of cups and saucers and a teapot that were grouped around the book. On the walls there
30 were some common coloured pictures, framed and glazed, of scripture subjects; such as I have never seen in the hands of pedlars, without seeing the whole interior of Peggotty's brother's house again, at one view. Abraham in red going to sacrifice Isaac in blue, and Daniel in yellow cast into a den of
35 green lions, were the most prominent of these. Over the little mantelshelf, was a picture of the 'Sarah Jane' lugger, built at Sunderland, with a real little wooden stern stuck on to it; a work of art, combining composition with carpentry, which I considered to be one of the most enviable possessions that the
40 world could afford. There were some hooks in the beams of the ceiling, the use of which I did not divine then; and some lockers and boxes and conveniences of that sort, which served for seats and eked out the chairs.

All this I saw in the first glance after I crossed the threshold –
45 child-like, according to my theory – and then Peggotty opened a little door and showed me my bedroom. It was the completest and most desirable bedroom ever seen – in the stern of the vessel; with a little window, where the rudder used to go through; a little looking-glass, just the right height for me,
50 nailed against the wall, and framed with oyster-shells; a little bed, which there was just room enough to get into; and a nosegay of seaweed in a blue mug on the table. The walls were whitewashed as white as milk, and the patchwork counterpane made my eyes quite ache with its brightness. One thing I
55 particularly noticed in this delightful house, was the smell of fish; which was so searching, that when I took out my pocket-handkerchief to wipe my nose, I found it smelt exactly as if it had wrapped up a lobster. On my imparting this discovery in confidence to Peggotty, she informed me that her brother dealt
60 in lobsters, crabs, and crawfish; and I afterwards found that a heap of these creatures, in a state of wonderful conglomeration with one another, and never leaving off pinching whatever they laid hold of, were usually to be found in a little wooden outhouse where the pots and kettles were kept.
65 After tea, when the door was shut and all was made snug (the nights being cold and misty now), it seemed to me the most delicious retreat that the imagination of man could conceive. To hear the wind getting up out at sea, to know that the fog was creeping over the desolate flat outside, and to look at the fire,
70 and think that there was no house near but this one, and this one a boat, was like enchantment.

I was very sensible of my entertainer's goodness, and listened to the women's going to bed in another little crib like mine at the opposite end of the boat, and to him and Ham hanging up

75 two hammocks for themselves on the hooks I had noticed in the roof, in a very luxurious state of mind, enhanced by my being sleepy. As slumber gradually stole upon me, I heard the wind howling out at sea and coming on across the flat so fiercely, that I had a lazy apprehension of the great deep rising in the night.

80 But I bethought myself that I was in a boat, after all; and that a man like Mr Peggotty was not a bad person to have on board if anything did happen.

Nothing happened, however, worse than morning. Almost as soon as it shone upon the oyster-shell frame of my mirror I was

85 out of bed, and out with little Em'ly, picking up stones upon the beach.

You work for a company which rents out holiday properties. It has bought the house on the beach and wants it to appear in its next brochure.

WS60 **1** Imagine that you have been to visit the house in order to make notes about it so that the company can advertise it effectively.

List the features which might appeal to your audience in a table like the one below. You will also need to invent some details which do not appear in the text; for example, Dickens does not mention a kitchen. Be imaginative with these extra details, but make sure they are appropriate to the setting: for example, you could appeal to a reader's sense of adventure by having the cooking facilities outside on the beach!

Part of house	Things to describe	Descriptive words
Outside appearance	black barge	charming, quaint
Main room	table Dutch clock	
Bedroom 1 In the stern (the back) of the boat	little bed	
Bedroom 2 At the front of the boat		
Kitchen (be inventive!)		
Outhouse	made of wood	
Situation	in Yarmouth on the beach	peaceful

WS61 2 Now use your notes to write the text which will go in the next brochure (you could include a picture of the property if you wish). Remember that the **purpose** of the text will be to **persuade** people to rent this property for a holiday. You will need to think about the other areas you have studied in this unit, especially your intended audience, the tone and the language that you use.

Note

Remember – this should be a persuasive piece of writing, so you should make the property sound appealing to your intended audience.

Unit summary

In this unit you have learned:

- When writing to persuade, the two most important elements are **audience** and **purpose.**
- There are a number of **language** techniques which you can use to make your persuasive writing more effective.
- **Presentational devices** can also be used to enhance your writing.
- **Facts** and **opinions** can be used selectively to make a point.
- Negative features can be made to sound positive if you write persuasively.

Activity

You have a large pile of second-hand housebricks in your garden. Rather than just taking them to the local refuse disposal centre, you have decided to try to make your fortune by selling them!

Using all your persuasive writing skills, create an advertisement in the form of a leaflet or poster which will persuade people to buy your product. Try to make your housebricks seem an irresistible bargain – the more imaginative your advertisement, the better. For example, you could advertise them as new-age ear-rings, or ornamental paperweights. You could use illustrations to spice up your advert.

Remember to have an audience in mind before you begin to plan your advertisement, and to think about the areas covered in this unit.

A9 Argument

What is an argument?

An argument is not just about two or more people disagreeing, or about who can shout loudest, or who can give a 'quick' or 'clever' answer.

It can also be about putting forward a point of view in a convincing way:

- I think this ...
- I think it because ...
- Having considered all the information, I think ...

A good argument of this sort consists of a point of view that is clearly set out, supported by evidence and reached after considering all the information and other viewpoints.

When you are 'writing an argument', you are composing a piece of writing in which you put forward your point of view, and your reasons for holding it. This unit teaches you how to structure your writing so as to do this effectively.

Examining the information

In order to develop and support an argument you need information.

The information given in the two leaflets on pages 102–5 is about the same topic – foxhunting.

The first is called *'Foxhunting – the Fiction and the Facts'* (see below and page 103). It is published by Countryside Alliance. The leaflet tries to persuade people to support foxhunting in Britain.

Information on foxhunting has never been hard to come by. Yet the public remain largely ignorant of what actually goes on. Perhaps this is because there are some very persistent myths about the sport, many of them inventions of a small but vociferous professional anti hunting lobby.

They say that:
- Foxes are not pests
- Foxes could control their own numbers
- Most people are opposed to foxhunting
- Hunting is irrelevant to conservation
- Foxhunting is cruel

In this leaflet, these statements are compared with the reality.

Foxes are not pests

Opponents of hunting claim that foxes do little or no damage and therefore do not need controlling. However, their claims are all based on research into fox populations which are **already** controlled. It is hardly surprising that the fox damage they find is less than it might be.

Even controlled fox populations still cause problems. A survey financed by the Countryside Alliance showed that in spite of control, 30% of farmers had experienced significant loss from foxes in the preceding twelve months.

This figure is supported by the research of an eminent Oxford biologist, Dr David Macdonald, who also found that the percentage of farmers believing that foxes should be controlled varied between 82.2% in the Midlands and 96.2% in the sheep rearing districts of Exmoor. Remember, too, that free range poultry are on the increase again.

Nor is the fox merely a pest to farmers. Game rearers and wildlife managers suffer serious fox predation on species of ground nesting birds, from grouse and pheasants to gulls, terns and waders.

Foxes could control their own numbers

Whilst it is obviously true that the breeding success of any species will be depressed by overcrowding, starvation and disease, it cannot be shown that foxes "control their own numbers" at a level where no damage will occur. Indeed the starvation factor can, by definition, only come into play after severe predation of available game and stock has taken place.

Most people are opposed to foxhunting

Hunting is an issue that does not affect the daily lives of the majority of British people, who are mainly urban based. Few have actual experience of the activity or understand its role in rural life. Therefore it is not surprising that many, misled by animal rights propaganda, are opposed to it.

The second leaflet, on pages 104–5, is called 'Foxes and Foxhunting'. It was published by the League Against Cruel Sports, who would like to see foxhunting banned.

Both leaflets claim to be presenting the facts about foxhunting. Read them both and consider the different points of view they present.

But it is questionable whether "most people oppose hunting". In fact when asked in a recent poll if hunting should be made a criminal offence, only 47% of people – less than half – agreed. In another recent poll, 59% of the public thought the continuation of hunting should be a decision not for Parliament, but for each individual landowner.

What opinion polls can't measure is strength of opinion, but it is clear that this belongs to supporters of hunting. Countryside March in 1998, brought about by attempts to ban hunting, was attended by more than 300,000 people. The most recent anti-hunting march attracted just 2,000.

Hunting is irrelevant to conservation

Foxhunters have never claimed they are the be all and end all of conservation but it is simply foolish to pretend that hunting does not have a beneficial effect on the landscape and the wildlife it supports. In some parts of the country its value is principally in contributing to the control of the predator. In other areas it acts as a brake on the pressures of commercial land management. Foxhunting farmers all over Britain maintain and plant scrubland, woodlands and hedgerows. Some hunts in places where fox habitat is scarce own hundreds of acres of ground cover in order that they know where they can find a fox on hunting day. Their action benefits many other species of wildlife in these otherwise bleak landscapes.

Banning hunting would not leave foxes unmolested but instead it would lead to an increase in their control by other methods. Foxhunting must therefore be compared not with some imaginary fox paradise but with the alternatives of trapping, snaring and shooting, which are legal, already exist and are necessary. These alternatives, in the hands of experts, generally result in a clean kill. However, used by inexperienced operators, they can cause suffering. Gassing and poisoning, though they cannot legally be carried out, would also increase.

Hunting's unique advantage is that the fox is either killed outright or the fox gets away totally unscathed. Even abolitionists now agree that the actual kill is extremely quick. The argument therefore rests on whether foxes suffer more by being chased than by the alternative methods of control. Hunting people believe that, on balance, being out of breath, or even very tired, involves less risk of physical suffering than the alternative.

In these terms, hunting is not cruel and from the fox's point of view it is better that it should continue.

Countryside Alliance

Is the fox a pest?

Each spring when fox-cubs are born, the fox population of Britain may reach half a million individuals. It is obvious that if foxes were a serious threat to agriculture, half a million of them would cause devastation and havoc. The fact is that most of the fox's feeding habits are not detrimental to farming – on the contrary, their predation on rabbits, rats and voles, all of which are considerable pests on the 70% of farmland given over to arable production, is of positive benefit to the farmer. Foxes also eat earthworms, insects, beetles, and fallen fruit as well as usefully scavenging the carcases of wild and domestic animals and birds.

With around 98% of poultry confined in intensive farming systems, it must be a rare fox which ever gets the opportunity to taste chicken, but they will take advantage of badly housed poultry and have very occasionally been known to steal free-range hens in daylight. However, the provision of sound night roosting sheds for the birds and a little electric fencing is usually enough to prevent such problems.

According to the Ministry of Agriculture, predation on lambs by foxes is 'insignificant'. Studies show that even by farmers' estimates, only one in two hundred lambs fall victim to a fox, whereas between 10% and 24% of lambs die from hypothermia, malnutrition or disease, or are still-born. Foxes carry away such casualties and are often seen in the lambing fields hoping to scavenge afterbirth. Because of this, foxes are ideal scapegoats for bad husbandry or lazy shepherds.

No escape for this fox

Foxes must have a year-long supply of food, so it follows that scavenging at lambing time would not affect the overall fox population density.

If a fox (often known as a 'rogue') does become a nuisance to a farmer, the animal can be selectively shot or caught in a humane cage-trap. However, it is better to protect vulnerable stock rather than to kill foxes, because if a vacuum occurs, other foxes will simply move in to fill it.

Fox meets cat in suburbia

Fox Ecology

The fox, like all predators in nature, has its numbers governed by the availability of food and the establishment and defence of territories. Man kills many tens of thousands of foxes annually, but vixens produce enough cubs to bring the numbers back to the density appropriate to the availability of food and territory. Fox killing merely produces an unnaturally young fox population; the actual numbers of foxes remain the same.

A survey carried out by Dr Stephen Harris of Bristol University in 1987 revealed that foxhunts kill between 12,000 and 13,000 foxes a year. Dr Harris points out that this may represent only 2.5% of the fox population, whereas fox populations can survive an annual mortality rate of up to 70% and still recover. Dr Harris concluded that, *"It is clear that foxhunts play no significant role in the control of fox populations."* In other words, 12,000 foxes die annually for no other reason than 'sport'.

Left alone by man, fox populations will be higher in areas of abundance of food and lower where food is scarce. This can be seen in towns and cities, where large numbers of foxes survive on refuse and high rodent populations. A 3-year study by Aberdeen University showed that in the absence of any form of fox control, there was neither an increase in fox numbers or in the number of lambs lost.

Foxes form stable family groups which defend their own territory against intruding foxes, and which will reproduce at a similar rate to their fatalities. The fox population would therefore not explode if all methods of fox killing were suspended. Surplus fox cubs, usually dog foxes, leave the home range when mature and seek to form or join new family groups in vacant territories. Most will be quickly accepted into groups depleted by perhaps a road accident, or human predation, while others may spend a considerable period as 'itinerants' before finding a new territory.

The public face of foxhunting

Foxhunting

Foxhunting has the same purpose as the now illegal pastimes of dogfighting, bear baiting and cockfighting – to provide amusement for human beings. It is not a form of fox control, nor is it meant to be. The 'control' argument was recently invented to counter the protests of those of us to whom the killing of animals for amusement is morally unacceptable.

Foxes mate in January and cubs are born in the spring. Foxhunting continues through the winter into April and occasionally even May. It is obvious therefore that not only pregnant and nursing vixens are hunted and killed, but also the dog-fox, on whom the vixen and cubs often rely for food. Every year, thousands of fox-cubs are orphaned this way and many die of starvation or are picked up and taken to animal shelters.

Foxhunters block up earths and badger setts the night before the hunt to ensure that foxes are forced to run until exhausted. Foxhounds are specially bred to run more slowly than the fox, but they can sustain a prolonged chase; accordingly the fox can outrun the hounds until it is exhausted and the bigger and stronger hounds are then able to catch it.

The longer the fox can keep up its efforts the more so-called 'sport' is obtained; therefore a weak, elderly or pregnant fox provides only a short hunt. A young, fit and strong fox can last up to two hours before it succumbs to fatigue, but the hounds can run for six or seven hours if necessary. If fast running dogs such as greyhounds or lurchers were used to hunt foxes, the whole thing would be over in seconds, but then there would be no 'sport'.

Foxes are not a natural prey species and have never suffered predation as a governing factor on their population density. The distress suffered by a prey species must be considerable when pursued by a predator, but the trauma must be far greater for a fox, not naturally adapted to endure long periods of pursuit.

Even if the fox manages to find an unblocked earth or badger sett in which to hide, the 'sportsmen' will either 'evict' the terrified quarry with terriers so that it can be hunted again, or if it is too exhausted to 'bolt', the terriers keep it under attack until the hunt servants and terrier men can dig it out and kill it. The death itself, though violent and painful, may be relatively quick. However the real cruelty of foxhunting lies in the exhaustion, terror and trauma inflicted on the victim.

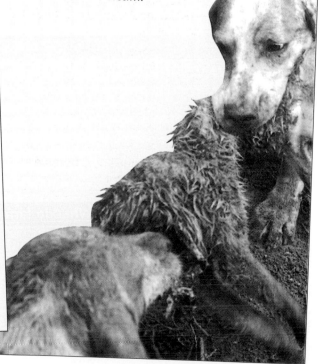

League Against Cruel Sports

Organizing the information

The writers of the two leaflets have very different views about whether the fox is a pest or not. In order to focus on this particular argument a little more, write down the points of view and evidence put forward by each side.

If you are to put forward a convincing argument in support of either view, you need to structure your information clearly at this stage. It will then be easier to structure your writing later on.

Activities

 1 In a table like the one below, give each organization's response to the questions:

- Do foxes attack chickens?
- Do foxes attack sheep?
- What do farmers think of foxes?

ARE FOXES PESTS?	
Countryside Alliance	League Against Cruel Sports
Do foxes attack chickens?	
Do foxes attack sheep?	
What do farmers think of foxes?	

There are two other major questions to which the two sides respond rather differently:

- Would foxes control their own numbers if they were not hunted?
- Is the hunt itself a cruel or humane way of killing a fox?

WS63, 64 **2** Using two more tables like the ones below, write down the **arguments** put forward by each side, together with the **evidence** that they give to support their arguments.

WOULD FOXES CONTROL THEIR OWN NUMBERS IF THEY WERE NOT HUNTED?	
Countryside Alliance	League Against Cruel Sports

IS THE HUNT ITSELF A CRUEL OR HUMANE WAY OF KILLING A FOX?	
Countryside Alliance	League Against Cruel Sports

Forming your own point of view

You need to consider **different points of view** when you write an argument. The aim of completing the three tables was to look carefully at two very different opinions about foxhunting.

The next thing that you need to do is to decide on your **own** point of view, having read the arguments on each side.

Are you *in favour* of foxhunting or *against* it?

When you have decided, you are ready to look at how to structure your writing.

Structuring your writing

Activities

1   First, look at the sort of words and phrases that will be helpful when you are doing this type of writing. These will all help you to compare one view with another.

however	alternatively	despite this
as for	on the other hand	to balance this
equally	nevertheless	to turn to
on the contrary	but	whereas
the opposite	for all that	all the same

When you have looked at the words and phrases:
  • try to think of an example of how you could use each one
  • suggest any other words or phrases like these that might be useful.

2 Next, you need a framework for your writing. Look at the plan below.

FOR / AGAINST

In your opening paragraph you need to state your *own* point of view

FOR	AGAINST
On balance, I am in favour of foxhunting, because I think there are strong arguments for it.	I am very much against foxhunting. I think it is cruel and unnecessary, because foxhunters kill foxes only for 'sport'.

Continue your essay by putting forward an argument for a view that is the opposite of your own. This gives you a chance to *answer* that opinion later on.

FOR	AGAINST
Some people, such as those in the League Against Cruel Sports, argue that foxes are not pests.	Foxhunters argue that foxes are pests and their numbers need to be controlled.

Explain the **evidence** that is put forward to support that opinion

FOR	AGAINST
They claim that foxes eat only rats, voles and other pests, rather than lambs and chickens.	They suggest that 30 per cent of farmers lose livestock every year due to foxes.

Then, go on to put forward the view that *you* hold about that particular aspect of the argument. You are **comparing**, so use phrases like '*However,*' and '*On the contrary,*'.

FOR	AGAINST
On the contrary, I believe there is evidence that foxes are great pests to farmers.	However, I do not accept that foxes are pests at all.

Give **evidence** to support your point of view.

FOR	AGAINST
Last year, 30 per cent of farmers reported 'significant loss' of livestock due to foxes, and foxes also kill wild birds.	Indeed, they hunt pests like rats and voles, and despite the myth, only 0.5 per cent of lambs are killed by foxes.

Repeat the process for each of your next points.

Writing the argument

Activity

 WS65, 66

Now you are ready to complete your piece of work. Choose one of the essays that have been started below and continue it. Use the information from the three tables you made on pages 106–7 to complete the essay.

Remember to add a concluding paragraph that summarizes your point of view.

An argument in favour of foxhunting

On balance, I am in favour of foxhunting, because I think that there are strong arguments for it.

Some people, such as those in the League Against Cruel Sports, argue that foxes are not pests. They claim that foxes eat only rats, voles and other pests, rather than lambs and chickens.

On the contrary I believe there is evidence that foxes are great pests to farmers. Last year, 30 per cent of farmers reported 'significant loss' of livestock due to foxes, and foxes also kill wild birds.

An argument against foxhunting

I am very much against foxhunting. I think it is cruel and unnecessary because foxhunters kill foxes only for 'sport'.

Foxhunters argue that foxes are pests and their numbers need to be controlled. They suggest that 30 per cent of farmers lose livestock every year due to foxes.

However, I do not accept that foxes are pests at all. Indeed, they hunt pests like rats and voles, and despite the myth, only 0.5 per cent of lambs are killed by foxes.

Writing an argument from scratch

In the work on foxhunting, the information was given to you. If you are asked to put forward an argument in a SATs test, the information would also be given to you. However, it is important to practise gathering your own information, for this will be a particularly important skill as you progress through school.

Activity

You are now going to 'open up' your approach to writing an argument. Your task is to write an argument from scratch. To do this you will need to:

- decide on a topic
- gather your information
- organize your information
- decide on your point of view
- structure your writing
- draft and write your argument.

Follow the steps below to help you to develop and write your argument.

Step 1: Decide on a topic

Choose one of the twelve topics below to investigate, or think of your own. Note that each topic is in the form of a question – so you know at once that there will be more than one point of view about the answer.

If you choose to investigate your own topic, put it into a question so that your readers know that they will be hearing arguments for and against a particular point of view (even though they will have to read the introduction to know what that point of view is).

- Is crime on the increase in Britain, or is it merely reported more often?
- Is alcohol the most damaging drug in use in Britain today?
- Is bullying a serious problem in today's schools?
- Does vegetarianism offer a healthier lifestyle?
- Space exploration – important scientific research, or a huge waste of money?
- Does global warming really pose a threat to the world?
- Should euthanasia be made legal?
- Is gambling harmless fun or a destructive menace?
- Do men and women have equal opportunities in Britain today?
- Is Britain really a 'classless society'?
- Is football violence a thing of the past?
- Does television help to educate us or merely waste our time?

Step 2: Gathering information

Think about where you might go, and what you might do, to investigate different points of view about it. For example, you might find information by:

- talking to people
- asking people to complete questionnaires
- visiting the library
- looking up material in encyclopedias (including CD-ROM encyclopedias)
- reading newspapers and magazines
- surfing the Internet.

You need to be precise about what you are going to do. Make a plan, in which you work out what you need to do to find out about this topic, and how you plan to do it. For example:

- Who will you interview?
- What key words and phrases will you look up? (Where? CD-ROM? Encyclopedia?)
- What magazines might provide you with information?

Once you have decided how to gather the information, start collecting it!

Step 3: Organizing the information

As you have seen, tables are a very useful method of organizing your information.

Draw up a table which allows you to draw together particular points of **comparison** or **contrast** easily. For example:

Is gambling harmless fun or a destructive menace?

Fun	A menace
Lottery – Statistics from Camelot re: average amount spent per week. Discuss how charity benefits.	Lottery – story from Daily Mirror re: woman from Exeter who had to sell her house – scratch card addiction.

You may end up with two or three tables as you did with the foxhunting materials.

Step 4: Decide on your point of view

Having listened to the views of different people, having read the books and newspaper articles, etc., what do you feel about the topic? Make up your mind about *your* point of view before you start to move on to the writing.

Steps 5 and 6: Structuring and drafting your writing

You should now use the material from your tables, and write out a first draft of your argument. Remember to follow the framework given on page 109.

When you have completed your first draft, and have checked your spelling, punctuation, etc., look again at the **structure** of your argument. Ask yourself these questions:

- Does it match the framework on page 109?
- Have you provided evidence to support your ideas?
- Does the argument progress logically?
- Have you made direct comparisons and contrasts?

Unit summary

In this unit you have learned:

- An argument can be about putting forward a point of view in a convincing way.
- How to **gather** information, so that you can listen to and consider different points of view.
- How to **organize** the information, so that you can compare information directly and see how arguments can be developed.
- How to form your **own** point of view.
- How to **structure** your argument.

B1 The English Key Stage 3 tests (SATs)

The exam

In May of Year 9 you will take the English Tests which will assess your reading and writing.

Paper 1 which lasts 1 hour 30 minutes (plus 15 minutes reading time) and is divided into three sections – A, B and C:

- Sections A and B test your **reading**
- Section C tests your **writing**
- You may be able to use some information in the first two sections to help you answer Section C.

Paper 2 which lasts 1 hour 15 minutes.

- You only have to answer **one** question about your Shakespeare text.

In this book we have been primarily concerned about your **writing**, but the areas you have covered in the units should also help you with your understanding of the various types of texts which will be found in Sections A and B of Paper 1.

Writing good answers

When you answer Section C in Paper 1 or the Shakespeare task in Paper 2, you will find it helpful to follow these simple guidelines:

1   **Read through the task** carefully two or three times to make sure you fully understand it.

2   **Before you write anything down**, ask yourself the following two questions:

- *Why* are you writing?   = **Purpose**
- *Who* are you writing for? = **Audience**

If you keep thinking about these two words in your writing (and in your responses to the other two sections), you will be on the right track!

3   **Write a plan:** *You will be assessed on your ideas and the way you organize and express them.*

You will not have time to re-draft your work as you did in class but a detailed plan will help you to organize your thoughts more carefully, may well save you time and gain you extra marks in the long run!

4　**Don't panic** if you make a mistake. Simply cross it out neatly.

5　*Remember that you will be assessed on your ability to write clearly, using paragraphs and accurate grammar, spelling and punctuation.*

Make sure you write in complete sentences, that your writing is organized in appropriate sections and that it makes sense.

6　**Check through your work** carefully when you have finished. You could save yourself some marks by correcting careless errors.

The following pages contain some typical Section C writing tasks. Each one is preceded by a piece of text to which it is connected, just as in the real tests.

B2 Test practice 1

Section C

This section of the paper is a test of writing. You will be assessed on:

- *your ideas and the way you organize and express them*
- *your ability to write clearly, using paragraphs and accurate grammar, spelling and punctuation.*

Study the leaflet from WWF – World Wide Fund For Nature and then choose **ONE** *of the following:*

EITHER

a) Your class has agreed to raise money for WWF.

Write a letter to parents of your year group explaining what you plan to do.

You could include:

- reasons why you want to support WWF
- the activities you are hoping to organize to raise money
- how you want parents to support your activities.

This is a formal letter, so you need to include a school address. Begin your letter 'Dear Parents'.

OR

b) Imagine that a pair of rare European wolves has escaped from a nearby safari park.

Write a front page report for your local newspaper.

You could include:

- details of the escape
- comments from local residents and the police
- views of the owners of the safari park
- plans to capture the animals safely.

OR

c) Animals feature in many stories. Sometimes they are given names, personalities and even dialogue!

Write a chapter in a novel which deals with the events in question b.

In your writing you could:

- try to convey the tension and excitement of the escape
- give the reactions of the wolves to the outside world
- include dialogue between the animals.

The end

is in sight

An urgent appeal from WWF

D. Lawson/WWF-UK

Black Rhino numbers reduced from 60,000 to 2,500 in less than 20 years

Chris Harvey/WWF-UK

There are more Asian elephants in captivity in Thailand than in the wild

D Underwood/WWF-UK

D Lawson/WWF-UK

Only 5,000 tigers left in the wild

Native Red Squirrel disappeared from much of England

Thousands of species lost every year

These are the facts. We can't afford to ignore them. We must act now to protect our vanishing species.

WWF

WWF-UK, Panda House, Weyside Park, Godalming, Surrey GU7 1XR   Registered Charity No. 201707   98HAB2

♻ 100% POST-CONSUMER WASTE

At the turn of the century there were more than 100,000 tigers

Now there are around 5,000

We may be looking at our last chance to save the tiger

D. Lawson/WWF-UK

These species all face extinction. Will you support the WWF campaign to help protect these and other threatened species and habitats?

WWF, the world's largest independent conservation organisation, is leading the fight for our vanishing species.

Campaigns by WWF have already helped protect many species of animals, birds and plants. But we will need to apply the full weight of our experience, gained over thirty six years in the field, to the battle that is to come.

We have put together an ambitious programme of action. But we must complete it. For many of our vanishing species, it may be their only chance of survival:-

Black Rhino. Population decimated from 60,000 to 2,500 in just 20 years.

Chris Harvey/WWF-UK

Effective conservation programmes

In 1982, we started a Community Guards project in Namibia, working with local communities to protect wildlife. So far the project has proved to be a huge success, with numbers of elephant, springbok and mountain zebra all on the increase — and the numbers of black rhino actually doubling.

Currently we are creating four of the largest national parks ever, in the Russian Arctic, home to the polar bear and many other species.

But this is only part of our work. With as few as 5,000 tigers remaining in the world, WWF are working to protect the tiger from the threat of extinction. We already fund projects across nine countries, but more protection is urgently needed for the tiger and other endangered species.

The Brown Bear. Extinct in the UK since the 10th Century. Virtually extinct in Western Europe (only 8-10 now left in France).

PJ Banks/WWF-UK

Working with governments

Wherever possible, WWF works alongside governments to secure the future of species. Often the responsibility for a species' survival rests solely with one country, such as the golden lion tamarin in Brazil and the Sumatran tiger.

WWF will continue to pressure all governments to put in place effective conservation programmes to protect their wildlife, and can help by providing the necessary expertise.

International lobbying

Wildlife trade is controlled by CITES (The Convention on International Trade in Endangered Species). Under which countries are required to have laws to protect vanishing species. But these well-meant laws will only prevent trafficking if they are vigorously enforced.

For years, Yemen has been a market for rhino horn for use in ceremonial dagger handles. After years of intense lobbying, Yemen finally joined CITES in 1997.

WWF will be doing all we can to help the authorities put in place CITES recommendations.

European Wolf. Extinct in many European countries. Threatened in others. Only 25 left in Sweden and Norway.

PJ Banks/WWF-UK

Exposing the illegal trade

After months of painstaking investigation, TRAFFIC our highly effective wildlife trade monitoring network, uncovered the largest ever haul of tiger bones in India. There have been other successes too.

One of our 18 TRAFFIC offices is currently working in Taiwan to provide the hard evidence needed to stop the illegal trade in rhino horn.

Bringing the eco-criminals to justice

With the profits from their illegal trade, poachers and traders can hire expensive lawyers. Often they escape on a technicality. In India, the WWF-run Environmental Law Centre helps ensure that the case for the prosecution is watertight. We need more centres like this as a serious deterrent to traffickers.

The Blue Whale. There are only 460 left in the Southern Oceans.

Paul Coppl/WWF-UK

Changing attitudes

WWF is helping to curb demand for products from vanishing species, through radio and TV programmes in many parts of the world that alert people to the devastating consequences of their actions.

WWF is involved in public awareness activities in Far Eastern countries which use rhino horn and tiger bone in Traditional Chinese medicines. Working closely with local communities, we hope to change public opinion towards wildlife conservation.

Enlisting the support of local people

We cannot protect vanishing species unless we have the support of the people like Salamu Wazirl. He used to hunt forest buffalo in the Gashaka Gumti National Park Nigeria, but now helps to protect the species with his tracking and guide experience.

It's this community-led WWF approach that's proved to reap rewards.

WWF is working all around the world; fighting for our vanishing species. We can't fight alone. Please support this crucial work.

Mountain Gorillas live in the upland forests of Zaire, Rwanda and Uganda. Just 600 are left.

R Wiederkehr/WWF-UK

B3 Test practice 2

Section C

This section of the paper is a test of writing. You will be assessed on:
- *your ideas and the way you organize and express them*
- *your ability to write clearly, using paragraphs and accurate grammar, spelling and punctuation.*

Read the passage on pages 121–122, which comes from **Great Expectations** *by Charles Dickens and then choose* **ONE** *of the following:*

EITHER

a) **Write a description of a person that you fear, or once feared.**

   You could write about a real or imaginary person.

OR

b) Magwitch has escaped from a prison ship. In the nineteenth century, convicts were treated harshly. They were physically abused, had little food and were kept in filthy conditions.

   Write a five-minute speech for a local radio programme.

   Begin your speech with one of the following statements:

   In my opinion, we should severely punish the criminal ...

   OR

   In my opinion, we should help the criminal to reform ...

OR

c) Imagine that you were in the graveyard and saw the whole incident described in the passage.

   Write a formal statement for the police.

   In your statement you should:
   - describe the appearance of the two people that you saw
   - outline the sequence of events
   - describe the attitude and behaviour of the two people
   - try to make your report factual.

Pip, a young lad, is looking around an overgrown churchyard near his home, when he is startled by an escaped convict called Magwitch …

'Hold your noise!' cried a terrible voice, as a man started up from among the graves at the side of the church porch. 'Keep still, you little devil, or I'll cut your throat!'

A fearful man, all in coarse grey, with a great iron on his
5   leg. A man with no hat, and with broken shoes, and with an old rag tied round his head. A man who had been soaked in water, and smothered in mud, and lamed by stones, and cut by flints, and stung by nettles, and torn by briars; who limped, and shivered, and glared and
10 growled; and whose teeth chattered in his head as he seized me by the chin.

'Oh! Don't cut my throat, sir,' I pleaded in terror. 'Pray don't do it, sir.'

'Tell us your name!' said the man. 'Quick!'
15 'Pip, sir.'

'Once more,' said the man, staring at me. 'Give it mouth!'

'Pip. Pip, sir.'

'Show us where you live,' said the man. 'Pint out the
20 place!'

I pointed to where our village lay, on the flat inshore among the alder-trees and pollards, a mile or more from the church.

The man, after looking at me for a moment, turned me
25 upside-down, and emptied my pockets. There was nothing in them but a piece of bread. When the church came to itself – for he was so sudden and strong that he made it go head over heels before me, and I saw the steeple under my feet – when the church came to itself, I
30 say, I was seated on a high tombstone, trembling, while he ate the bread ravenously.

'You young dog,' said the man, licking his lips, 'what fat cheeks you ha' got.'

I believe they were fat, though I was at that time
35 undersized for my years, and not strong.

'Darn me if I couldn't eat 'em,' said the man, with a threatening shake of his head, 'and if I han't half a mind to't!'

I earnestly expressed my hope that he wouldn't, and
40 held tighter to the tombstone on which he had put me;
partly, to keep myself upon it; partly, to keep myself from
crying.

'Now then, lookee here!' said the man. 'Where's your
mother?'

45 'There, sir!' said I.

He started, made a short run, and stopped and looked
over his shoulder.

'There, sir!' I timidly explained. '"Also Georgiana."
That's my mother.'

50 'Oh!' said he, coming back. 'And is that your father
alonger your mother?'

'Yes, sir,' said I; 'him too; late of this parish.'

'Ha!' he muttered then, considering. 'Who d'ye live with
– supposin' you're kindly let to live, which I han't made
55 up my mind about?'

'My sister, sir – Mrs Joe Gargery – wife of Joe Gargery,
the blacksmith, sir.'

'Blacksmith, eh?' said he. And he looked down at his leg.

After darkly looking at his leg and at me several times,
60 he came closer to my tombstone, took me by both arms,
tilted me back as far as he could hold me; so that his eyes
looked most powerfully down into mine, and mine looked
most helplessly up into his.

'Now lookee here,' he said, 'the question being whether
65 you're to be let to live. You know what a file is?'

'Yes, sir.'

'And you know what wittles is?'

'Yes, sir.'

After each question he tilted me over a little more, so as
70 to give me a greater sense of helplessness and danger.

'You get me a file.' He tilted me again. 'And you get me
wittles.' He tilted me again. 'You bring 'em both to me.'
He tilted me again. 'Or I'll have your heart and liver out.'
He tilted me again.

*Eventually, Magwitch releases Pip, after making him promise to say nothing
and return with some food the next day.*

B4 Test practice 3

Section C

This section of the paper is a test of writing. You will be assessed on:
- *your ideas and the way you organize and express them*
- *your ability to write clearly, using paragraphs and accurate grammar, spelling and punctuation.*

Read the advertisement on the next page.

The advertisers are trying to persuade the audience to take a holiday in Cuba.

*Choose **ONE** of the following:*

EITHER

a) Imagine that you have been on the holiday to Cuba, and were very disappointed.

   Write a letter of complaint to the tour company.

   In your letter, you could outline:
   - the delays and discomforts you endured on the journey
   - the problems encountered at the hotel
   - what you want the tour company to do now.

OR

b) Imagine that you work as a holiday rep in Cuba for the company in the advertisement. Your job is to make sure that the people on holiday with your firm enjoy themselves and that you deal with any problems they may have.

   Write about what happens on a typical day.

   You could write a diary entry for the day. You could include:
   - different problems you encountered with your clients
   - how you solved these problems
   - your private thoughts on the holidaymakers.

c) **Write a description of a place that is important to you.**

   In your writing, you could use different senses to convey the atmosphere of the place.

Cuba

14 nights from £949

For all you've ever wanted in a holiday – and more ...

Come to Cuba...

5 With its miles of white sandy beaches, tropical climate and old world charm, Cuba is surely a paradise on Earth. Now you too can visit this island – the largest and most beautiful in the Caribbean – on our all-inclusive luxury tour.

We have a range of different types of holiday to suit every taste.

10 Whether you want to go scuba diving amongst the fishes in the blue-green Caribbean Sea, explore the mysterious forests and wildlife of the interior or just lie soaking up the sun on one of the world's most beautiful beaches at Varadero, we can provide the right package to suit every taste.

You will be based in four star comfort at the Hotel Las Grandas in Havana
15 with its old world charm and traditional architecture. The hotel, situated in the heart of this magical city, is equipped with its own swimming pool, bars, night club and fitness suite. There are crèche facilities available around the clock, and our friendly local guides are always on hand to advise and help ensure that you have ...

20 ## ...the holiday of a lifetime!

Our 14 day tour price includes: ∗scheduled flights from London, Heathrow ∗airport tax ∗13 nights accommodation, full board ∗sightseeing tours of Havana ∗boat trip to the beautiful Isla De La Juventud ∗scuba gear hire ∗bicycle hire ∗visits inland to the Montemar Great National Park and to a tobacco plantation in Pinar del Río province.

Glossary

adjective	a word which gives more information about a noun. For example, The **muddy** water.
alliteration	the repetition of consonants (letters other than a, e, i, o, u) in two or more words near each other. For example, **w**hispering **w**ind (see page 43).
audience	the person or people that the writing is for.
caption	a phrase which draws attention to a picture or illustration.
colloquial language	an informal or conversational style.
consonant	any letter of the alphabet which is not a vowel (the vowels are: a, e, i, o, u).
dialogue	conversation spoken by characters (see page 23).
direct speech	the actual words used by a speaker. For example, **'I am going home,'** said Nigel (see page 79).
directive language	phrases or sentences which give instructions or orders to the reader. For example, Go away! (see page 90).
emotive words	words which arouse strong feelings in a reader (see page 90).
eyewitness account	the report of someone who actually sees an event (see page 78).
fact	a statement which can be proved.
imagery	the use of words to create a picture in the reader's mind, usually by comparing one thing with another.
indirect speech	(see **reported speech** and **direct speech**).
metaphor	a type of image. The writer speaks of something as if it actually were something else. For example, He had the heart of a lion. The words 'like' and 'as' are not used, unlike a **simile** (see page 44).
narrative	the telling of a story (see pages 7 and 24-6).
non-Standard English	writing or talking in a relaxed, informal manner. For example, when writing a letter to a friend. (See also **Standard English**).
onomatopoeia	a word whose sound echoes its meaning. For example, hummed, thwacked (see page 43).
opinion	what someone believes.
paragraph	a section or passage of writing.

personal pronouns	words used in place of nouns. For example, *I, you, we* (see page 91).
personification	the writer speaks of a non-living object as if it were a person. For example, *Tulips **nodded** in the breeze* (see page 45).
plot	the events in a story in the order in which they happen.
purpose	the reason for your writing.
repetition	when the same word or phrase is repeated. Repetition is used by writers to make the reader take particular notice of something.
reported speech	the form of speech as it is reported, not as it was originally spoken. For example, *Nigel said he was going home.* (See also **direct speech**).
reporting clause	the words that tell you *how* a character says something. For example, *'I hate you!'* ***she screamed.***
rhetorical question	a question which does not require an answer. For example, *'How could you do this?'*
scene headings	in a script, these tell you where the scene takes place (see page 32).
setting	where events take place – the place, the time and so on (see page 14).
simile	a type of image. In a simile the writer *compares* something with another thing using the words 'as' or 'like' (see page 44). For example, *'The wind roared around the house like an angry beast.'*
stage directions	tell the reader how to read or act out the lines in a drama script. They also give other information about how the scene should be presented, for example, describing setting, props and so on.
Standard English	writing or talking in a formal manner without using slang expressions or abbreviations. For example, when writing a job application. (See also **non-Standard English**).
stanza	a verse in a poem.
tension	a sense of expectancy or excitement as the reader waits for something to happen.
tone	an overall mood or feeling of a piece of writing. For example, *serious, mocking, persuasive* and so on.
verb	often called a 'doing' or 'action' word. For example, *laughed, cried.*
viewpoint	the point of view from which the story is told.
vowel	the following letters of the alphabet: a, e, i, o, u.

Acknowledgements

The Publishers would like to thank the following for permission to reproduce copyright material:

David Higham Associates for the extract, 'The Ratcatcher', from *Someone Like You* by Roald Dahl, published by Michael Joseph, pp10–1; Egmont Children's Books Ltd, London for an extract from *The Ghost of Thomas Kempe* by Penelope Lively © Penelope Lively 1973. Published by Heinemann Young Books, an imprint of Egmont Children's Books Ltd, London and used with permission, p16; HarperCollins Publishers Ltd for an extract from *Wild Swans* by Jung Chang, pp17–8; Zahir Hussain for the extract on pp19–20; Egmont Children's Books Ltd, London for the extract from *Granny Was A Buffer Girl* by Berlie Doherty © 1986 Berlie Doherty, published in the UK by Methuen Children's Books and Mammoth, imprints of Egmont Children's Books Ltd, London and used with permission, pp24–5; Penguin UK for the extract from *A Kestrel for a Knave* by Barry Hines © Barry Hines 1968, published by Michael Joseph, 1968, p26; Colin Smythe Ltd for the extract (hardcover) from *The Colour of Magic* by Terry Pratchett © 1983 by Terry Pratchett, p30; Transworld Publishers Limited for the extract from *The Colour of Magic* by Terry Pratchett published by Corgi, a division of Transworld Publishers Ltd, © TM & Copyright 1992 Terry & Lyn Pratchett. Adaptation and art Copyright 1992 Innovative Corp. All Rights Reserved, p31; The Peters Fraser and Dunlop Group Limited for the poem 'Streemin' taken from *You at the Back* by Roger McGough © Roger McGough, p36; Bristol Broadsides for the poem 'Goodbye' by Carol-Anne Marsh, p36; The Society of Authors for the poem 'Silver' taken from *The Complete Poems of Walter de la Mare* 1969, reprinted by permission of The Literary Trustees of Walter de la Mare, and the Society of Authors as their representative, p36; Rogers, Coleridge & White Limited for the poem 'A Small Dragon' taken from *Notes to the Hurrying Man* by Brian Patten © Brian Patten 1969, reproduced by permission of the author c/o Rogers, Coleridge & White Ltd., 20 Powis Mews, London W11 1JN, p37; London Association for the Teaching of English for the poem 'Holiday' by Corolyn J. Turner, p40; Greenwillow Books for use of the poem 'Huffer and Cuffer' by Jack Prelutsky, taken from *The Sheriff of Rottenshot* by Jack Prelutsky Text: Copyright © 1982 by Jack Prelutsky, by permission of Greenwillow Books, a division of William Morrow & Company Inc, p43; Faber & Faber Ltd, for 'Winter' taken from *Midnight Forest* by Judith Nicholls, p46; Penguin UK for the extract from *Zlata's Diary: A Child's Life in Sarajevo* by Zlata Filipovic, translated by Christina Pribichevich–Zoric, (Viking 1994, First published in France as *Le Journal de Zlata* by Fixot et éditions Robert Laffont 1993) Copyright © Fixot et éditions Robert Laffont 1993, p59; Westworld International Ltd, for the extract from 'Mean Street Diaries' by Stephen Smith 1998, p60; BBC Worldwide for the extract from *Around the World in 80 Days* by Michael Palin with permission of BBC Worldwide Limited © 1989 Michael Palin, p60; Random House UK Ltd for the extract from *The Growing Pains of Adrian Mole* by Sue Townsend, p60; Hinchingbrooke School for the extract from *Simon's Diary*, p61; Cassell for the extract from *Flowers for Algernon* by Daniel Keyes © Daniel Keyes, pp63–4; International Masters Publishers Ltd for the text from the *Soccer Brilliance – Group 2 Card 29*, p68; National Express for the two National Express adverts, p69; Barnsley Metropolitan Borough Council (Elsecar) for the extract from 'Heritage Centre' leaflet, p70; Mid-Somerset Campaign for Nuclear Disarmament for the extract 'Leaving Zilch Behind' taken from *The Glastonbury Festival 1999* leaflet, p70; Boots The Chemist for the extract from their 'Give Up Smoking' leaflet, p70; Mattel UK Ltd for the extract from 'Junior Scrabble instructions' JUNIOR SCRABBLE ® and RAINBOW SCRABBLE ® are registered trademarks of J.W. Spear & Sons PLC, Leicester LE3 2WT, England, p71; Dept of The Environment, Transport and the Regions for the extract from 'A Highway Code for Young Road Users'. This is Crown Copyright, p72; *The Guardian* for the advert 'The SS Universe Explorer', 10.10.98 © *The Guardian*, p91; P91; Eidos Interactive Ltd for the advert for 'AKUJI' PlayStation game, p91; Mazda UK for the flyer to win a holiday in Chicago, p92; Corsican Places for use of the text from their advert for Corsican Places, p93; CIBA Vision UK Ltd for use of the text from their advert for *Focus Dailies*, p93; Jackson, Stops & Staff for use of the text from one of their adverts, p93; WWF-UK for use of the information from 'The Year of the Tiger', p94; Countryside Alliance for use of details from their leaflet 'Foxhunting – the Fiction and the Facts' Countryside Alliance, The Old Town Hall, 367 Kennington Road, London SE11 4PT Tel: 0171 582 5432 Fax: 0171 793 8899 HYPERLINK http://www.countryside-alliance.org www.countryside-alliance.org, 'The Countryside Alliance champions the countryside, country sports and the rural way of life', pp102–3; League Against Cruel Sports Ltd, Sparling House, 83–7 Union Street, London SE1 1SG Tel: 0171 403 4532 fax: 0171 403 4155, for extracts from 'Foxes and Foxhunting', pp104–5; WWF-UK for use of extracts from their leaflet 'The End is in Sight', pp118–9.

The Publishers have made every effort to trace the copyright holders, but if they have inadvertently overlooked any, they will be pleased to make the necessary arrangements at the first opportunity.

The Publishers would like to thank the following for permission to reproduce photographs on the pages noted:

Granada Television, p14; Peter Sanders, p20; Bridgeman Art Library, p62; Allsport UK Ltd, p68; Hulton Getty, pp85, 87; Tony Stone, pp93, 124.